S0-BCA-410

Heroes
and Horses

❧

Sept. 29, 2004

For Myra Tobin
with best wishes

Philip Ardery

Heroes and Horses

Tales of the Bluegrass

PHILIP ARDERY

THE UNIVERSITY PRESS OF KENTUCKY

Publication of this volume was made possible in part
by a grant from the National Endowment for the Humanities.

Copyright © 1996 by The University Press of Kentucky
Paperback edition 2004

The University Press of Kentucky
Scholarly publisher for the Commonwealth,
serving Bellarmine University, Berea College, Centre
College of Kentucky, Eastern Kentucky University,
The Filson Historical Society, Georgetown College,
Kentucky Historical Society, Kentucky State University,
Morehead State University, Murray State University,
Northern Kentucky University, Transylvania University,
University of Kentucky, University of Louisville,
and Western Kentucky University.
All rights reserved.

Editorial and Sales Offices: The University Press of Kentucky
663 South Limestone Street, Lexington, Kentucky 40508-4008
www.kentuckypress.com

08 07 06 05 04   1 2 3 4 5

The Library of Congress has cataloged the hardcover edition as follows:
Ardery, Philip, 1914–
Heroes and horses : tales of the Bluegrass / Philip Ardery.
p.   cm.
ISBN 0-8131-1992-8 (cloth : alk. paper)
1. Bourbon County (Ky.)—Social life and customs.
2. Bluegrass Region (Ky.)—Social life and customs. 3. Ardery, Philip,
1914–   4. Horse farms—Kentucky—Bourbon County. 5. Bourbon
County (Ky.)—Biography. I. Title.
F457.B8A73   1996
976.9'423—dc20   96-27941
Paper ISBN 0-8131-9115-7

This book is printed on acid-free recycled paper meeting
the requirements of the American National Standard
for Permanence in Paper for Printed Library Materials.

Manufactured in the United States of America.

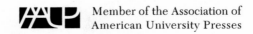   Member of the Association of
American University Presses

Contents

List of Illustrations vii

Acknowledgments ix

Prologue 1

ONE Rocclicgan 2

TWO The Folks at Home 11

THREE Bourbon County Boyhood 25

FOUR Horse Country 36

FIVE Ed Simms and Xalapa 48

SIX Claiborne Farm 56

SEVEN A Hero of World War I 68

EIGHT Prich 77

NINE Barton Stone and Cane Ridge 97

TEN Cap'n 110

Epilogue 118

Illustrations

Bourbon County Courthouse 3

Rocclicgan 6

William B. Ardery 13

The Ardery boys 18

Julia Spencer Ardery 21

Ardery Place and Duncan Tavern 23

The "Yellow Peril" 27

Head Play and Broker's Tip in 1933 Derby 39

Phil and Anne Ardery 43

Man O' War and Will Harbut 44

Ed Simms and James W. McClelland 49

Stone horse barn, Xalapa 52

Tower, Xalapa 53

Swale 57

Claiborne Farm 65

Reuben Hutchcraft 70

Ed Prichard, 1935 81

Ed Prichard, 1994 95

Central Christian Church 99

Old Cane Ridge Meeting House 101

Barton Stone 102

Cap'n 111

✤

Acknowledgments

My first expression of appreciation must go to Evalin Douglas, an outstanding editor. She smoothed out the major bumps in my bumpy writing, leaving the little bumps so those who know my deficiencies can identify what they see.

Then a host of others need mention. I remember with gratitude my talks about Claiborne Farm with Waddell Hancock; with her son and farm president, Seth, for many details; and with her artistic daughter, Dell, who provided photographs of that farm. Similarly, Lillie Webb of Xalapa Farm helped me with my work on Ed Simms and Xalapa.

The library staffs of the Lexington Theological Seminary, the Louisville Southern Baptist Seminary, and the Louisville Presbyterian Seminary helped me find many details for the story about Barton Stone and Cane Ridge.

Of course, no one could write about Bourbon County history without heavy dependence on the excellent reporting of the Lexington *Herald-Leader* and the Louisville *Courier-Journal*.

By the kindness of the editors of the thoroughbred magazine *Spur*, the Sunday magazine of the *Courier-Journal*, *The Filson Club Quarterly*, and the *Register of the Kentucky Historical Society*, I have been permitted to republish, in revised versions, articles or parts of articles they carried many months or years ago.

The rest of the credit goes to Anne, my wife, whose angelic patience has carried me over the many times when I became angry and dissatisfied with what I was trying to do.

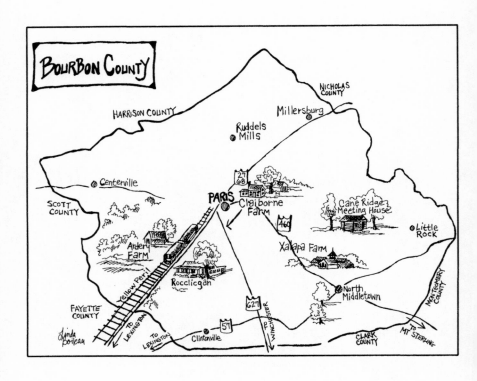

✦

Prologue

It is difficult for me to say how much is still with me that I learned about Bourbon County as a child. How much is left of the boy who lay belly-down chewing blades of bluegrass and heads of sweet white clover, or of the boy who bent over the high bank of Houston Creek to see the kingfishers wing in and out of their hole in the bank.

So much of the happiness of those days was somehow connected with water. There was the springhouse down across the road from our home where a clear stream of icy water came out of the ground and formed a pool framed with limestone slabs, then flowed through a hole in the brick wall and into the tiny shack. Inside, the water made a left-angle curve, then a right, and flowed out through another hole in the back wall. The back room was where we put pounds of butter and watermelons in the water to keep them cold.

The spring branch had its beginnings at the back of the springhouse and ran about half a mile till it emptied into Houston Creek. It was always alive with crawdads, minnows, and an occasional small, harmless water snake. Building a mud dam across it was great fun. The water would build up and up into a pool and finally trickle across the top of the dam. Next thing you knew, the whole mud pile would explode down the stream.

How many of those memories can I carry with me, and how much of that same child am I now? Perhaps some later experiences—like looking down the barrel of a 20 mm automatic weapon firing at me, or seeing pieces of an airman friend picked up from the ground and carried away in a basket—may have blotted out much of my childhood belief that things were basically all right and would never change.

ONE

Rocclicgan

Bourbon County, Virginia, was established by the Virginia General Assembly in 1785; Kentucky was not to become a state until seven years later. Out of Bourbon County were carved some thirty other counties of the present Commonwealth of Kentucky, north to the Ohio River and east to the Big Sandy. It was a wilderness then. The Ardery pioneers came into their land the easiest way—by marriage. My great-great grandfather John Ardery Jr. married Elizabeth McConnell on New Year's Day, 1818. Her father, William McConnell, had fought in the Revolutionary War and for his service had received more than a thousand acres of Bluegrass land by federal land grant. This was to make of the Arderys something close to landed gentry—Arderys whose ancestor William Ardery had left Ireland three generations earlier, grabbing for any opportunity he could find.

Kentucky today has a ridiculously large number of counties for a state of its size—120 in a total area smaller than its northern neighbor, Ohio, which has only 88. Among the 120, Bourbon County is average in size. Its population has been remarkably stable during my lifetime. The county population by the 1930 census was 18,060; fifty years later it was 19,405. Similarly, the population of the county seat, Paris, was 6,204 in 1930 and only 7,935 in 1980. During much of my youth, Paris was one of the leading markets for bluegrass seed and burley tobacco.

Bourbon Countians in my time took pride in the superiority of their educational system. Paris High School was especially strong in math and English, and a number of its graduates went east to Ivy

Bourbon County Courthouse in Paris, built 1902-5.

League schools. Princeton seemed the favorite of a number of my contemporaries.

Then, too, Paris, the seat of Bourbon County, was the birth-place and final resting place of John Fox Jr., born at Stony Point in Bourbon County in 1862 and buried in the Paris Cemetery in 1919. Fox was famous for stories about Kentucky—*The Little Shepherd of Kingdom Come,* said to be the first American novel to sell a million copies, and the very popular *Trail of the Lonesome Pine.*

One of the county's more infamous claims to fame is the origination of Bourbon whiskey. In pre-Prohibition days the county boasted many famous distilleries, but the question of who was the real inventor of the stuff is for Kentuckians to fight over. Anyhow, twenty-five Bourbon County distillers were indicted in the seven years from 1791 to 1798 for failure to pay the federal tax on their product. Thus, the long-standing American tradition of tax rejection, extending from the Boston Tea Party into the indefinite future, has part of its history in Bourbon County.

Several family names are prominent in the county—Clay, Woodford, Roseberry, Spears, Rogers, Simms, Buckner, and Hancock. (Note that Ardery was not among one of the more prominent names.) Intermarriage has resulted in a Woodford Spears, a Clay Woodford and a Woodford Clay, a Rogers Clay, and a Buckner Woodford as well as a Woodford Buckner. Everybody knows everybody, and most are cousins.

A life span or two can cover more than we think. "Cap'n," an old black man who as a child was a slave owned by my great-grandfather, told me that when he was a boy he once heard a "painter" scream. He meant a panther, the only truly American wild cat, once native to the land. "If you'd evah hyeerd a painter scream, you never forgit it." The scream, he said, came from a woodlot on a hill across the road from our house. Cap'n's life and mine together have covered a lot of history.

I was born March 6, 1914, in Lexington, Fayette County, just south of Bourbon County, and was brought home to a small house in Paris. Shortly after that we moved to a farm on the Paris-Lexington Pike, about four miles south of Paris, and there I spent most of my youth. Our family doctor, Will Kenney, used to say that any boy who grew up in Bourbon County and drank Shanty Spring water was bound to be a good man. Shanty Spring was down the road toward Paris, about a mile from our farm. Doc Kenney, one of the best loved citizens the county ever had, delivered more babies than any other Bourbon County doctor. As a consequence, there were white and black children all over the county named Will Kenney this and Will Kenney that.

The world around me began coming into focus when I was a little more than three years old. One of my earliest recollections is of walking hand in hand with my grandfather, William Porter Ardery, on the front porch of our house. He'd had a stroke and my parents were frightened he might fall on me. He was a huge man we called "Big Dad."

I have one way of fixing the time of my earliest recollections with some accuracy. My father took me to the Paris depot to see Jim Thompson, a black man who worked for us off and on, who was departing for World War I, so it must have been 1917. Jim wore a campaign hat and wrap leggings, the uniform of those days. I remember Jim waving to us out of the window as the train pulled out of the station.

My scanty recollections of the small house in Paris made the big house on our farm seem even bigger. The new place soon became a living, protecting, vital part of my life. The house was built of limestone quarried nearby and was situated on a bedrock foundation of the same limestone. "Rocclicgan" was the name Mother chose for our new home. I don't know where Mum came upon the name, but I was told it was Gaelic or Welsh and meant "built on a rock." It had a rock wall fronting the spacious, tree-shaded lawn, and at the front gate there were two pillars of stone with tall arbor vitae on either side. A long, semicircular gravel driveway ran up the hill from the main gate and down the hill and out another gate that also fronted on the Paris-Lexington Pike. Another part of the drive led to the garage beside and behind the house.

Rocclicgan was the central point of my early consciousness. When I was four, my father and mother were the mighty powers that ruled, but my father had his own life as a small-town newspaper owner/editor/publisher, a lawyer, a sportsman, a farmer, and a country gentleman. It was my mother who played the principal role in my life. Mum was the daughter of a clergyman. His denomination, the Disciples of Christ, was usually called the Christian Church. We called ourselves "Christians"; others called us "Campbellites," a mildly pejorative term taken from Alexander Campbell, one of the sect's founders. I remember a Bourbon Countian who said his uncle was a gentleman of the old school because he never called a Campbellite a Christian.

Campbellite or not, my mother's Christian influence on me was

Rocclicgan, built in 1913.

strong. She often took me to visit her father, who was the pastor of Central Christian Church, at that time the largest Protestant church in Lexington. His name was Isaac Jesse Spencer, and his wife, Louise, was a daughter of Dr. Philip Barbour Pendleton of Louisa County, Virginia. It was from him I got my name, Philip Pendleton Ardery.

In my grandparents' house we always said prayers and usually a short reading of scripture before meals. I was taught to say "Yes, ma'am," "No, ma'am," "Thank you, ma'am," and "'Scuse me." In later years, my grandmother Spencer laughed at my desire to do everything just right by following many of my actions with the whole thing: "Yes, ma'am, no, ma'am, thank you, ma'am, 'scuse me."

I must have been six or seven years old when it was agreed by all, including me, that I should be baptized. The whole family went to the Paris First Christian Church and were met by Brother Ellis, the minister. I was dressed in an immaculate white linen suit, shirt and tie, and properly shined shoes. Brother Ellis was in a formal claw-hammer coat and striped pants. He asked me if I thought I knew what it meant to be baptized, and I said I did. Then he asked me if it was my desire to be baptized and was I prepared for it. I said yes. Then he took me to the baptismal pool in the church, a sort of oversized marble bathtub filled with water about waist deep. He put his arm around my back, held a linen napkin over my face, and pushed me all the way under as he said, "I baptize thee in the name of the Father and of the Son and of the Holy Ghost."

My father was an Episcopalian when he met my mother. She swung him into her church, which was very important to her. Years later, when I married, I reversed my father's action by leaving the Christian Church to become an Episcopalian like my wife. Someone asked Mum if she was upset at my having become an Episcopalian, and she replied, "Of course not. Phil has been totally immersed and he'll be all right."

But back to Rocclicgan. It was a wonderful house. It had three great fireplaces, and bedrooms for each of three young boys, in addition to the master bedroom. It also had a large kitchen, a dining room, a living room, a front porch, and a sunporch in the rear.

The kitchen was my main point of interest as a little boy. Across from the large coal range was a long table made of boards. It was covered with an oilcloth that hung over the sides. When the servants, usually two or three, were "gettin' supper," I would crawl under the kitchen table, where I felt warm and secure. The help knew I was there, of course, but they paid me no attention; I was too young to be noticed. I loved to hear their conversation, unintelligible to most white grown-ups but quickly absorbed by a child. Its music and humor and picturesque expression made white talk seem flat and colorless.

When Clara, our cook for many years, was at the peak of her labors, she and the others would often sing songs that seemed to me the most beautiful I had ever heard. Or someone would begin to whistle in a way quite different from the way most whites whistle. The soft notes would snap sharply from one pitch to another rather than slide. I learned to whistle and use my tongue to snap note changes and trill the way blacks did. I can still do it but not as well as I could sixty years ago. So I realized early in life that black people had a vivid culture of their own.

Part of that culture was a kind of wry humor well illustrated in a story my mother used to tell. One time when she was having a party, she put Jack, the son of our cook, in a white jacket to make him look like a formal houseboy. She handed Jack a fly swatter and told him to go out on the back porch and swat flies. After he'd been there about half an hour, Mum went to see how the operation was coming along. Jack was sitting in a chair, the swatter idle over his knees. "Jack," she said, "I thought I told you to swat these flies. This place is just black with them." "Yas'm," was the reply. "Miss Julie, I done awready hit most of em onct but they jus lies on they backs and looks at you till you go away, then they gits up and flies off."

I loved Jack and the other "colored people" around the house and farm, but once I got into trouble by using the word "nigger" in earshot of my mother. She was furious; she grabbed me by the collar and said, "Don't you ever use that word again." I responded with some surprise, "They use it to each other all the time." Mum said, "That doesn't make any difference; you are not to use the word, and if I ever hear it from you again, I'll take you to the bathroom and wash your mouth out with soap." Some years later, in a serious moment, she said, "Phil, I want you to know something about colored people. We white people have treated them miserably for two hundred years. Their day will come, and when it does, I want you to remember we've got it coming to us."

The blacks in our house gave me great joy and taught me many things about life. I once heard one of the black men say to his wife, "You got to do this," to which she responded, "No, I ain't got to do nothin' but die." That truth has stayed with me.

One of the Rocclicgan rituals that I found most exciting came in the early evening when Cap'n, pushing a wheelbarrow, would bring in ten or twelve gallons of milk produced by our cows. He would carry the big milk cans down to the cellar and start the task of separating it into cream and skim milk. The separator had a great tub-like top that held the milk. When the handle was turned, the milk would trickle through the machine into a fast-spinning centrifuge. The lighter cream would come out one spout and the heavier skim milk out another. The cream would be put into earthen crocks to go into the icebox (in later years, the refrigerator). The skim milk would go back into one of the large milk cans to be taken down to the pig lot in the back and poured into a large wooden trough for our pigs, along with potato peelings and other edible garbage from the kitchen.

The squealing and shoving pigs excited me. It always seemed unfair for one big pig to put his foot in the trough and use his shoulder to keep his smaller brother or sister out. I usually kept a stick to whack the big ones and sort of even things out.

The house felt almost as much a part of me as a turtle's shell is part of the turtle. In the cellar, besides the room with the cream separator, there were a large coal furnace, a coal pile, and many dark corners filled with mysterious pipes and valves. In a separate room were three rows of batteries and a gasoline engine that powered a generator. This was the Delco System. There was an electric power line a short distance from the front of the house, but the Kentucky Utilities Company would sell power only to the interurban streetcar line that ran parallel to the highway. Residences were not served, hence our need for the Delco System to generate our own electric power. The cellar opened onto the back yard by steps going up to slanting cellar doors.

The attic was even more exciting. It held trunks full of old letters with funny one-cent stamps on them and a big old roll-top desk. The desk held many wonders, including considerable currency of the Confederate States of America, thought to be worthless but still possessing a mysterious contingent spark of value.

One of the most painful days of my life was the day the principal of the Paris school had me called out of class. My father had telephoned to say the house was on fire and I should come home. I don't remember where my brothers were, but I do remember catching the next interurban street car. When the car came over the hill at a little settlement called Monterey, I could see a pillar of black smoke and red flames reaching skyward through the trees from Rocclicgan. The motorman stopped at our front gate and held the car so all the passengers could ogle the Ardery family tragedy in progress. Furious at such morbid curiosity, I ran up the driveway with tears streaming down my face.

There were people standing around in the yard. Some of the furniture had been taken out and stood naked on the lawn. I don't recall looking for my mother or father or brothers. I walked down the lawn and across the pike, crying my heart out. It was as if a member of the family were dying, calling me for help, and I could do nothing. Life could never be the same; I knew it.

Later, my father put us all in the car and took us to the Windsor Hotel in Paris. Eventually Rocclicgan was rebuilt, but the scar from my memory of the fire never left me.

TWO

✦

The Folks at Home

My father, William Breckenridge Ardery, was born in 1887, the only child of William Porter and Ellen Adair Ardery. He married Virginia-born Julia Spencer in 1910. He was twenty-seven when I, his third son, was born. My brothers and I, when we were small, called him "Dits"; later I called him Dad. I must have been around three or four years old when my memories of him begin. I recall his taking me up in front of him in the saddle as he rode his mare across the farm. With 365 acres, our farm seemed to me a vast estate. We had two and, for a time, three tenant farm families to grow tobacco, corn, and hay (and earlier hemp), and to take care of the cattle. My father did little farming but spent a lot of time tending a large garden in which he produced everything from sweet corn to immense strawberries.

Dits was probably the best educated Ardery up to his time. He held A.B. and LL.B. degrees, which he earned after graduating from a private preparatory school. Although I studied Latin in high school and college, my Latin could never match his. He also knew some Greek.

He was always interested in politics and was a staunch Democrat. As a legislator for about ten years from the late '20s, he became a respected leader in Kentucky's lower house. One thing he did in the legislature I especially enjoyed. He succeeded in laughing out of consideration an attempt to legislate into Kentucky law some of the nonsense that cropped up in Tennessee and gave rise to the Scopes "monkey trial." A bill was proposed in the Kentucky House to forbid the teaching of Darwin's theory of evolution. Dits

11

introduced an amendment that would require water to run uphill. At this, the know-nothings gave up.

Dits also went into a section of Bourbon County where a resurgence of the Klan was strong to speak on behalf of Al Smith for president in 1928. As a consequence, he suffered politically for many years. I must have been in the eighth grade when one boy in my class, proud of his Klansman father's 100 percent Americanism, would dance around chanting:

> I'd rather be a Klansman
> With a robe of snow so white
> Than to be a Catholic
> With a robe as black as night,
> For a Klansman is an American
> And America is his home
> And he does not have to kiss the toe
> Of the Jewish Pope at Rome.

From a Klansman's point of view, that says it all.

Up until the Depression, Dits was more or less a member of the idle landed gentry. He had a law degree and was admitted to the bar but never practiced. His father had left him a principal stockholder of three small-town banks. He also owned and published the Paris *Democrat,* which was widely read and enjoyed, mainly because of the leprechaunish humor in a column he wrote titled "WBA," for William Breckenridge Ardery.

Dits was not only a good writer but an admirer of good writing. More than fifty years ago, on my birthday, he gave me a compilation by Arthur Krock of editorials by Henry Watterson, the famous editor of Louisville's *Courier-Journal.* I opened the cover and saw inscribed there, "To my youngest son—a true Kentuckian. Dits." Here is a sample of Marse Henry's eloquence, from an editorial written December 25, 1868. Watterson was decrying the federal government's policy toward the former Confederate states. He began by describing a meeting of backwoodsmen, including Daniel Boone and James Harrod, on December 25, 1778. On a high cliff overlooking the frozen Kentucky River, they knelt and prayed, sang

William B. Ardery as a young man.

a hymn and adopted a resolution commending the patriots who were "fighting the battles of freedom beyond the mountains." Noting that Kentucky had never seceded from the Union, Watterson continued:

> The snows of nearly a hundred years have come and gone since the Christmas of 1778. Many a change has come also over the land. The canebrakes are all gone. The old pioneers are all gone. Their graves are deep-sunken under the ploughshare, and are hid beneath the clover blooms. But the hardy manhood; the warm, impulsive love of freedom; the honest hatred of persecution; the keen sympathy with the weak and suffering, all these noble sentiments that honored the lives of the fathers remain and are illustrated by the children in the unanimity with which they resist the despotism set up over their brothers at the South. Remove this despotism, and we may divide on a thousand issues; but as long as

it continues we are one in opposing it as unnecessary, tyrannical, and cruel.

Dits was a great fly fisherman and hunter and took me with him many times to watch admiringly as he fought a black bass with his tiny flyrod, or made a double with his shotgun when two doves flew over his stand in the shooting field. He was an expert marksman, and not just in the eyes of a small son. I have a yellowed clipping from the Paris paper showing that in 1927 he ranked fourth in the state in trapshooting averages—not bad against rural Kentucky competition.

When I was ten or eleven years old, Dits bought me a Remington .22 caliber semiautomatic (then called an automatic) rifle for Christmas. He was quite strict about it and gave me detailed instructions about how to handle it: Always carry it barrel down under the right arm, so any accidental discharge would go harmlessly into the ground well away from the right foot. Always keep the safety on until ready to fire. When aiming, never close one eye, as so many of the unknowing think proper; keep both eyes wide open looking directly at the target. When the target is seen clearly, bring the sights into line. And don't kill song birds. Birds on the allowable kill list were mainly birds one could eat—doves, blackbirds, and pigeons. Also killable were jays, sparrows, and crows. Crows got our baby chicks when they first hatched, so crows could go.

Even when I was shooting them, I had an increasing fondness for jays, and now the recollection that I shot so many of them pains me. They make gossipy whispering sounds to each other up in the leafy tops of the trees. But when sounding an alarm at the presence of a cat or some other predator, they put their heads down and scream, "jay! jay! jay!" This is clearly an obscenity in the jay language. They have another flutey call that sounds like "tru-lee, tru-lee." When the jay gives this call, he rocks up and down on his heels and points his head up. Jays have an interesting streak of meanness in them, but they're also truly beautiful, with their little topknots, black collar ring, and blue and white wings and back. They're a perfect example of God's greatness in design. One writer, Walter

Havinghurst, calls the jay "a flying flower." Dits grew more and more tender-hearted about all living things as he got older, just as I have. If he were alive today, I'm sure he would put blue jays on the protected list.

I was never as good a marksman as he was, but that's how—quite a few years later—I got my criminal record. By that time I was a student at Harvard Law School, home for a vacation just before school began again, and Dits took me along for a dove shoot. This was the first dove season since passage of the federal Migratory Game Bird Act, which made it a crime to hunt over a baited field. But we gave no thought to whether the field where we would be shooting was baited or not. When we got there, we saw some turkeys scratching around and feeding but paid no attention to what they were feeding on. We took our places in the field and the shoot began. Dits was under a big ash tree and when he had killed three or four birds, Raymond Connell, a fellow hunter, found a dead robin which he stealthily hid in Dits's pile of birds. More birds came in, and when Dits had about ten birds and I had maybe three, a stranger entered the field and walked up to Dits (who was by this time the circuit judge of our district). The stranger identified himself as a federal game warden and asked to see our hunting licenses. Then he checked the pump guns to see that they were "plugged" so they could hold no more than three shells. Dits always shot a Parker double gun.

The warden then started counting Dits's birds to be sure he hadn't killed more than the limit, which, as I recall, was twelve. About the fourth bird he came to was the dead robin. Raymond Connell and I were standing off to one side enjoying Dits's chagrin at the sight of the robin. Obviously not knowing he was talking to the circuit judge, the warden said, "What kind of a goddam sportsman do you call yourself, anyway, killing a song bird?" At that point Raymond intervened to tell the warden that he had found the bird dead under the tree and had just slipped it in with the doves as a joke. A careful look at the robin convinced the warden that that was true. But he also found hempseed, the current bait for doves, scattered around. He gave us citations to answer in federal court in Lexington. It appeared that one of the neighbors who had wanted an invitation to the hunt but hadn't received one had turned us in.

We decided it would be unwise to tell Mum what had happened. But in a few days the Lexington *Herald* carried a story about how Judge Ardery and City Attorney Connell and others had been hauled into court, booked and fingerprinted, and fined as violators of the Migratory Game Bird Act. Mum hit the ceiling, and we were in the dog house for a long time, particularly so because the day after the story was printed, I delivered a "back to school" sermon at the Paris Christian Church.

Our interest in sports wasn't limited to the rural pastimes of shooting and fishing; probably our greatest preoccupation was horse-racing, about which more later. This was long before small-town life became identified with high school rivalries in football and basketball—even longer before the electronic media brought national sports competition into every living room. Nevertheless, when I was nine years old, Dits was greatly excited over the Dempsey-Firpo fight to be held September 14, 1923. We had no radio then, of course, so Dits got all of us in the car at a proper hour of the evening to ride to town and get the news of the fight. I cannot exactly recall how the news came in, perhaps by wire service. In any event, as we neared the center of town, people were shouting from the street, "Dempsey won!"

Next day the paper carried the story, telling in astonishing detail how the Argentinean Firpo, "The Wild Bull of the Pampas," in the first round knocked Dempsey through the ropes and completely out of the ring into the laps of some of his ringside fans. Dits seemed a bit hurt by this. I remember him saying, "He'd never have made it back into the ring before a count of ten if some of those fans hadn't thrown him back in, and that wasn't at all fair to Firpo." Whether that was true or not, Dempsey won in the second round by a knockout. He had knocked Firpo down ten times and been knocked down twice in a fighting time of less than four minutes, beginning to end.

Another form of entertainment was a special joy to me, largely because it was my exclusive privilege as the youngest child. In the

Paris schools, students in the fifth grade began having classes all day. After my brothers reached that point, I was still getting out at noon. So in my third and fourth grade years, when I rode the interurban home, I often found Dits and Mum waiting in our Oldsmobile touring car to take me to Lexington. We'd go to the Ben Ali theater, named for Ben Ali Haggin, a wealthy landowner and horse breeder, and there we'd see a movie and full vaudeville show. There was almost always a blackface act with a Mistah Bones responding to comments made by Mistah Interlocutah, with dancing, banjo, and tambourines—always the same but to me highly entertaining. There was always a magician who caused me to vow that I'd be a magician some day. And there was the inevitable dog act. Nobody had to explain to me in later years the saying "Never follow the dog act."

My privileged status as a small boy is probably reflected again in my memory of blackbird pie, which I read about in Mother Goose and confidently asked Mum to make for us. She gave orders to my father to bring some blackbirds, which he did, after exercising his prowess as an expert with his shotgun. He didn't bring in four-and-twenty, but perhaps a dozen. These Mum cooked. Then she put them in a big pan lined and covered with pie crust, which was then browned in the oven. When the pie was opened, the birds didn't begin to sing, but it was truly a delicious meal, fit to "set before a king." An accomplished cook, Mum went into the kitchen whenever we got a new cook and taught the newcomer all the intricacies of culinary art—good southern cooking, but no grits and no greasy foods. Often she did her job of teaching so well that our cooks would be hired away by wealthier Bourbon County matrons.

Mum played the piano in the family orchestra, which included my brother Bill on the saxophone and my brother Win on drums. Bill was almost exactly three years older than I. He was a natural leader, one a younger brother could look up to. Bill and I seldom fought, although I remember one time on the farm when I had gathered a basket of fresh eggs in the hen house; I got irked at Bill about something and started throwing eggs at him. He just laughed and dodged. I must have smashed a dozen eggs and never hit him once.

At Paris High School, Bill was looked up to by all the boys but

The three Ardery boys, Bill, Phil, and Win, about 1918.

became something of a problem for the school administration. He had a way of sneaking out of class to play pool at Paris's main pool hall (known among the students as "the study hall"). When Bill turned up missing, Professor Scott, principal of the high school, would dutifully put on his hat and coat and walk to the "study hall," hoping to make the catch. One afternoon Bill was in a study hour in a classroom on the ground floor when Professor Scott, who was monitoring the students, stepped out for a minute to visit his office down the hall. Bill quickly opened a window and jumped out. He then waited and watched around the back of the building until he saw Professor Scott, hat and coat on, heading out to the "study hall." Then Bill slipped back in and sat down in his seat. Some time later when the professor returned, Bill was deeply absorbed reading an appropriate textbook.

My brother Winston was a year and a half older than I. As a boy he was handsome, blue-eyed, and blond. He was what we called "feisty." We fought a great deal at one period of our lives, and I never won a single encounter. I was known as a bit of a crybaby and a 'fraidy cat, neither of which Win was. But we had many good times together. One time in Paris, when a considerably larger boy attacked me, Win climbed him from behind. When the boy turned on Win, I picked up a rock and hit the guy in the back with it. He made one more turn toward me and was jumped again by Win, at which point the bully figured he'd better take off.

For all the sparks that flew, there was a considerable bond of affection between Win and me. One of the many incidents I remember with affection concerned my treasured microscope, a very low-powered one that I had saved up to buy from Sears Roebuck. I was out in the yard with Dad one day, having given Win permission to use the microscope. Suddenly Win burst out of the house, crying and saying, "I've broken the microscope." I thought he'd broken the lens. I rushed into the house and knelt beside the small instrument, almost in a state of shock, only to find that Win had lowered the scope onto the slide holding the dead fly or whatever it was he was looking at, so that it broke the slide. The lens was intact. With considerable relief I assured Win he had done no real harm; slides were no problem.

One day when Win was fifteen, he was working in a chemistry laboratory at the high school. Someone working beside him was heating a glass vial over a Bunsen burner when there was an explosion, and a bit of glass entered Win's eye. He lost the sight of that eye. When it became apparent that his injury was permanent, my father got us together and made us both promise we'd never fight again. We never did.

Some of my memories of Win are tinged with sadness. I remember one time when we were quite young, perhaps five or six. Win and I found a bottle of whiskey (very fine bonded bourbon, as we were to hear later) hidden in a closet at home. It was winter. We went out to the little pond in the corner of our front yard, broke a hole in the ice over the pond and poured half the contents into the

hole. Then we filled the bottle back up with water and returned it
to its original hiding place. About a week later all hell broke loose.
It was all Mum could do to keep Dits from firing our cook, Clara,
forthwith, so sure was he that she had been drinking his whiskey.
Win and I wouldn't have wanted to lose Clara, but we kept abso-
lutely quiet. To little boys it all seemed very funny, but later we
would come to know alcohol as a family problem. Dits was able to
put it behind him, as did Bill. I had my own difficulties, yet managed to keep working until retirement. But Win, the gentlest and
most likable of the Ardery boys, died a victim of alcohol a few years
ago, even after years of success as a certified public accountant.

When the Great Depression came, Dits's three banks all went
broke, and the *Democrat,* though popular, had never made money,
so Mum took over management of the family business affairs. Because of the bank failures and other adversities common to millions
of Americans at the time, the People's Deposit Bank of Paris sought
to foreclose the mortgage on our farm. Mum was outraged. She
didn't realize that a paper she had signed some years before gave
up her dower right in the property and gave the bank a right to
foreclose. The sheriff actually came and tacked a piece of paper on
the front door of our nice big house, indicating that the place was
up for public sale.

Mum fought foreclosure with a vigor that was more than the
bank had anticipated. She had been doing paid genealogical work
for years and had earned a reputation in the field. She convinced
the bank that my father would somehow get a job and she would
consistently earn enough so the bank would get monthly payments
sufficient to cover the loan. She did increase her work load and I
suppose made $100 to $150 a month, which was a good sum in
those days. About that time, our commonwealth's (district) attorney died, and the governor appointed my father to fill the vacancy.
Suddenly we switched from being a family of idle landowners to a
family headed by two pretty good money earners. Dad rose from
near zero as a courtroom lawyer to a respected position as advocate
for the Commonwealth of Kentucky against criminal offenders.

Mum, as a consequence of her research on families, compiled

Julia Spencer Ardery.

Kentucky Court and Other Records in two volumes. The books sold well and were highly regarded as an authoritative source of Kentucky family history. Later, when my oldest son, Peter, was approaching college age, I took him to visit Harvard, Yale, and Princeton. The first thing he wanted to do was go to the libraries and see if he could find his grandmother's books. Sure enough, they were there.

Mum's fighting spirit came out on other occasions, too. I guess I had gone off to law school when the Paris City Council proposed to demolish Duncan Tavern, a dilapidated stone structure on the courthouse square, unused for many years. The tavern was built in

1788, and many of the early pioneers had lodged there, including the famous Simon Kenton. It stood on a hill just above the big spring that had first attracted settlers to the place that became Paris. The settlement was first called "Hopewell." Local tradition said that was because pioneers coming through the Wilderness Trail from Cumberland Gap to Lexington said to each other, "Hope we'll get there before dark." Actually, Hopewell was the New Jersey hometown of one of the founders. Later the name was changed to Paris, to go with the French-inspired name of the county.

Mum consistently saw beauty many others did not in the history of Bourbon County and in the Duncan Tavern. She asked for a special hearing before the city council, and convinced the council that if they would let the building stand, she would one way or another find the money to restore it. Her idea then was to turn to the Daughters of the American Revolution, in which she had been prominent for years. Bit by bit, at her urging the DAR put up money for Mum to hire a stonemason here, a carpenter there, and a painter somewhere else. For a small fraction of what it would have cost had a contractor done the job, she orchestrated and superintended the whole restoration herself. Today Duncan Tavern stands magnificently at the top of the hill behind the courthouse, one of the most beautiful historic relics of the beginnings of Paris. I suppose it was Mum's work that, along with my father's record of more than thirty years as a circuit judge who sat in the main courtroom of the courthouse, led the city to name that part of the square "Ardery Place."

My father never lacked courage, as he showed in 1944. I had finished one combat tour flying bombers in Europe in World War II and was on a thirty-day leave to the States before returning. Dits, a heavy cigarette smoker most of his life, had developed a hoarseness that he didn't seem able to shake. As soon as I heard him speak, I asked him if he'd seen a doctor. He said, "No, it's nothing. I don't want anything to spoil your trip home, but I'll go as soon as your leave is over." "In that case," I said, "I'm leaving tomorrow unless you see a doctor tomorrow."

He reluctantly agreed. A biopsy showed cancer of the larynx.

Phil Ardery, with Duncan Tavern in the background.

Dr. Fred Rankin, a widely known surgeon in Lexington, recommended surgery by a Dr. Maurice Buckles.

Dr. Buckles explained to me how persons who have had laryngectomies learn to talk again by swallowing air and regurgitating it so as to use the esophagus as a substitute for the vocal cords. Dits stayed in the hospital for a day or two to determine what was to be done, but he told me he didn't want any such operation. He was fifty-seven years old and said he'd led a happy and fulfilled life and would rather let cancer take its course.

I left him at the hospital and told him I'd be back the next day. The next morning I spent about an hour walking around the field back of our house swallowing air, regurgitating it, trying to make words. I became convinced that what Dr. Buckles had said was right. That afternoon I had a big smile on my face as I entered Dits's hospital room. "I did it!" I almost shouted at him. Then I belched a word. I tried it several times with enough success to convince Dits that it could be done.

He had the operation and learned to talk again well enough to go back on the bench. Microphones were installed for the first time on the benches of his courtrooms in Paris, Georgetown, Versailles, and Frankfort, and he remained a successful circuit judge for twenty-three more years until his death near the age of eighty. More than once, persons facing the same operation came to sit in his courtroom to hear him and take courage from his courage.

THREE

Bourbon County Boyhood

Bourbon County in my early recollection was heaven. Its gently rolling hills were green and gracious. It had racehorses and cows and chickens and dogs. We were not racehorse people, but we usually had a saddle horse or two, which my father loved to ride, often taking me up in front of him in the saddle on his favorite mare. The salty, musky smell of saddle leather and horse sweat was pure joy.

My brother Win and I sometimes played a game called chicken. We would take wood shingles from a bale of them kept in the barn for repairing roofs, trim the heavy end down with a knife into a sort of handle, and make little holes in the paddle end to let air through so it would be an effective bee swatter. Then we'd go to a place in the heavy clover and bluegrass of the front lawn where we'd previously spotted a nest of bumblebees. Win or I would kneel down beside the nest and swat bees one by one as they came in or lifted out of the grass. Almost every time, after a few swats, the swatter would miss a bee, and that was the signal to take off in a hurry. After a few moments the other would take position over the hive. The winner was the one who could stay in place the longest.

Little boys and bumblebees were natural enemies in those days. We couldn't see any sense in bumblebees. They could sting again and again, unlike honeybees, which died after stinging once. Besides, honeybees made honey and therefore served a useful purpose. What good was a bumblebee? My father answered that by telling us a story. Some Kentucky red clover seed had been exported to South Africa and planted there. The clover grew but wouldn't spread. At last they solved the problem by importing bumblebees. The heavy bumblebee could pollinate the clover better than any

other kind of bee. My father thought red clover was one of our greatest blessings, much greater than white clover, timothy, alfalfa, les-
pedeza, or any other similar feed crop. At that time, many
thoroughbred owners wouldn't feed their horses any kind of hay
except red clover. So we really needed bumblebees.

About 150 yards in front of the house and our stone gateway
was the Paris-Lexington Pike. On the far side of the pike was a rail
line that linked Paris with Lexington and four other Central Kentucky towns. Long, orange-yellow interurban cars traveled up and
down the line, and there was a stop right at our front gate.

We called the cars the Yellow Peril. My brothers and I, for a
few pennies a trip, rode the interurban almost every day of our lives
until we graduated from Paris High School. Like the Kentucky Utilities Company, the local electric-power distributor, the interurban
line was owned by the Kentucky Traction & Terminal Company in
Lexington, a subsidiary of Middle West Utilities. Middle West was
a top holding company of the Samuel Insull utility empire head-
quartered in Chicago.

The Yellow Peril connected Paris with the Bluegrass towns of
Nicholasville, Georgetown, Versailles, Frankfort, and Lexington. In
the beginning it operated on electric power the company produced,
but later it retired its generators and bought power from Kentucky
Utilities. Like so many Insull companies, its original stockholders
in May 1911 included some of the most prominent local business-
men, each holding three shares of stock, and the Kentucky Securi-
ties Corporation, another Insull subsidiary, holding some 19,000
shares. What, if anything, each of these shareholders paid for his
three shares, I have not been able to learn.

You'd think we'd have loved those interurban cars, but somehow they aroused the kind of animosity in me and my brothers as
little boys that automobiles do in dogs. We figured out many ways
to persecute the interurbans just because of their presence in our
lives. Win and I would board the car to go to school in Paris and
most often would go to the rear smoking section, which was sepa-
rated from the front of the car. In the smoking section there was a
small room with a toilet letting out directly onto the rails below,

The "Yellow Peril."

obviously not to be used while the car was standing in the station. The design of the toilet was such that one could feed toilet paper down it so the paper would go out the bottom while remaining attached to the roll of paper beside the toilet seat. We could fix it so that when the car entered Paris it would trail a floating, flapping festoon of toilet paper.

Win and I would get off a stop before the car got to the end of the line and walk the couple of blocks to school, arriving about the time the motorman was pulling into the station. People on the street would be laughing at the festoon of toilet paper. That was part of the saga of the Kentucky Traction & Terminal Company's Yellow Peril.

Another part of that saga was a great plan I dreamed up—and I count myself lucky that I didn't land in jail for it. I had noted with some interest the operations of the Louisville & Nashville Railroad about a quarter of a mile behind our house. Workmen, pulling themselves along on little pump-up-and-down handcars, would often stop and move their car off to a small platform beside the track, then take their picks and other tools down the track quite some distance, frequently out of sight of the car. Having watched them work and signal trains, I knew that under the seat of the handcar was a box containing small red-paper-covered explosives. These had small strips of lead attached to bend around the track and hold the gadgets in place so that a wheel passing over them would be sure to set them off.

As I recall, two of them placed a few feet apart signaled a locomotive engineer to slow up; a single one placed some way farther down the track meant "Stop." On at least two occasions my friends and I just happened to be walking down the track after a crew of workmen had parked a handcar and disappeared around the bend. Seeing the coast clear, we lifted several of the small explosives from the car and disappeared. The next scene found us in the early evening hiding in a clump of tall horseweeds in front of the one-room school up the hill from our house. We had clamped three of the purloined contraptions onto the interurban track. There we waited anxiously for the arrival of a car. The line at that point was on a fairly steep downgrade, and we were confident the motorman, driving at his accustomed speed, wouldn't be able to stop.

Then came the Yellow Peril around a slight curve and down the hill. The interurban had two sets of brakes. One pair was a shoe type that, when applied, simply rubbed on the wheels. These were the brakes for normal operation. The others, emergency brakes, were magnetic; when applied, they dropped heavy bars down to rub the track. When the car hit the three explosives, great sheets of flame flew from under the wheels, and we heard a triple thunderclap that carried easily half a mile. Mr. Motorman simultaneously hit his regular brakes and his magnetic brakes. The jolt almost threw all the passengers out of their seats. He stopped the car, got out and looked all around, and having satisfied himself there were no more explosives, got back in and slowly moved down the hill.

The recollection of those episodes is the thing that continues to make me patient and sympathetic with dogs that bark at my car and little boys who throw mud balls.

The Yellow Peril was a wonderful part of our lives and would be a great thing today, if Central Kentucky had it back, to save energy and bind together the Bluegrass. Sam Insull was considered a great villain when his utilities empire collapsed, carrying with it the fortunes of many. In 1932 he fled to Europe. He returned and faced trial in 1934 and was acquitted of all criminal charges. But the Kentucky Traction & Terminal Company went bankrupt in 1934 and paid Kentucky Utilities $655,500, which was forty cents on the dollar it owed for power.

The last interurban car left Paris for Lexington on January 13, 1934. The line had performed a great service for twenty-three years. I am one to witness that, whatever else he was, Samuel Insull was a real builder, and the Yellow Peril and other systems like it were well worth it all.

Squire Benjamin Redmon and his large family lived in one of our tenant houses at the top of the hill toward town, in a small settlement known as Monterey. I can't exactly remember how many children there were, probably around eight. My main chums were twins my age, Willie and Bob, and Jouett, whom everyone called Jupe, a year or so younger. Then there was the oldest boy, Charlie, who was about four years older.

Charlie was considerably bigger and stronger than the rest of us and was given to demonstrating his superiority in such ways as twisting our arms up behind our backs, throwing us on the ground and generally making an ass of himself.

One day we were down on the creek bank just above the deep hole where we swam. We had a plan we were eager to try out to get even. Charlie happened to be there, and Bob told him that if he would lie down on his back I could put my hands under him and lift him straight up off the ground. As we had expected, Charlie met this with ridicule. But the other boys swore they'd seen me do it, and after a certain number of "betchas," Charlie agreed to prove how silly the idea was. He lay down on the grass, and we told him to stretch his arms and legs out so the others could "steady him" and keep him from falling off my hands. My brother Win got hold of one arm while Willie and Bob and Jupe grabbed the other arm and his legs. "All set!" I called out. Then I quickly unbuttoned helpless Charlie's fly, pulled out his prick, and spit on it. An instant later, the five of us broke, running in five different directions, as the livid, red-faced Charlie got up and with liberal profanity buttoned up his pants.

In my path, a short distance from the scene of the crime, was a sagging barbed wire fence. I tried to clear it without breaking stride, but one of the barbs caught my pants leg and ripped it all the way down. If I had been half an inch lower, it would have gotten my ass. Anyhow, Charlie never caught any of us, but from that time on he had as little to do with us as possible.

Win didn't seem to share my interest in having a kind of club with the Redmons. But from age six to about twelve, Willie, Bob, Jupe, and I were almost daily companions, especially during the summer months when school was out. The Redmons tended a crop of tobacco and had to work hard; I was their unpaid helper. I learned how to plant tobacco from a tobacco setter, a vehicle pulled by two mules that carried a big drum filled with water, where the driver sat. There were two low-slung seats at the back between which hung burlap bags filled with freshly pulled tobacco plants. As the contraption moved along, the part of it between and slightly in front of the two-seated planters would make a little furrow. Then there would be a click as first one planter and then the other put a plant in the ground. Each time it clicked, a cupful of water would be released into the furrow to give the plant a good start in dry soil. Besides planting tobacco, I learned how to "chop out"—that is, to hoe the weeds out, to "sucker" (remove suckers), and to cut and house and strip.

Willie Redmon was a wonderful, happy boy with a wide, handsome face. He and I had about the same outlook on most things. In our long summer days outdoors in the fields, it was natural that I should start a collection of Indian arrowheads. I found a great many in certain pastures on our farm and especially on one hillside of a neighbor's place. But the best one I had was one Willie gave me. It must have been about five inches long, gracefully tapered to a very sharp point and notched at the back. The flint was white and almost translucent. I never shall forget how thrilled I was when he gave it to me. Later I learned that Willie had traded his prized Barlow knife to get it from another boy.

Willie once told me he'd "heerd" the most valuable thing in the world was a "gold diamint." When Willie and Bob went to Paris to see their first "moompicturshow," I knew something great would come of it. Sure enough, when they got back Willie could hardly wait to tell me about it. It seems there was this pioneer—or maybe he was a cowboy—who was alone on the prairie, building a camp-fire in the late twilight. On the scene behind him crept five Indians, tomahawks in hand. The first Indian tiptoed up to our hero and raised his tomahawk for the kill. Suddenly the pioneer-cowboy came alive, grabbed the red arm that held the weapon, and threw the assailant over his shoulder and into the roaring fire. "And don't you know that sombitch whupped all five of 'em!" Willie's eyes were round with amazement as he related the story. It certainly was enough to inspire courage in the hearts of thousands of young Americans. I could imagine the guy in the piano pit playing while the fight went on.

The tobacco crop was usually taken to market in the late fall or early winter—most of it was sold between Thanksgiving and New Year's. I well remember one year's sale. It was 1928, the year the first Model A Ford came out. Squire Redmon took his share of the proceeds of his crop, almost in its entirety, and bought Charlie a sparkling new Model A Roadster. When my father heard about it, he was upset and went to the Redmon house to talk to Squire. Later Dits told us what happened. He got Squire out behind the house and out of earshot of the rest of the Redmon family and told him he had done a terrible thing. He said Squire told him at great length about how Charlie, as a little boy, had labored with him on the farm from dawn till after dark. Charlie had never gotten anything for helping feed the family. Squire was crying when he told the story. My father put an arm around him and said, "I understand."

Dits rarely interfered in my personal life, but on one occasion he did, during the time the Redmons and I had our gang. A new farm boy named Banford Adams had moved into the neighborhood. It was obvious he wanted to play with us, but I decided he shouldn't be admitted to our circle, that we should have nothing to do with him. He was oversized, ungainly, and seemed unusually stupid. We must have tortured the poor fellow for some weeks when somehow it got back to Dits what was going on. "Why won't you play with that Adams boy?" he asked me. "I think you're being mean. I wish you'd put yourself in his place and think of how you'd feel." Dits's comment shamed me, and I went immediately to search out Banford. From then on he was a full-fledged member of the gang.

The Redmons were wonderfully ingenious at finding ways to entertain themselves. I learned from them how to take wires and bend the ends of them into a "v" to push small steel wheel rims from which the spokes had been removed. We pretended these were racing cars. The hooked wire would push and guide the small hoop forward or make turns to the right or left, to the great joy of the child running behind. We also loved getting inside a worn-out, discarded automobile tire to roll head over bottom down a hill into the spring branch. There was never a lack of things to do. At Paris High School, a wonderful English teacher, Miss Noland, once told me with a twinkle in her eye that she had heard I would stay up past midnight, when everyone else in the house was asleep, looking at the Sears Roebuck catalogue. It was true, but I was embarrassed by the thought that others talked about me that way. I guess lots of farm boys became similarly addicted. I remember one of my friends commenting about a certain pretty lass, "She's as sexy as the corset section of a Sears Roebuck catalogue."

I enjoyed the corset section, but I also enjoyed the parts of the catalogue offering musical instruments, binoculars, cameras, sporting goods, and a whole host of other things. The catalogue provided a cornucopia as accessible as the mailbox down by our front gate. That is, of course, if one had money for the net price and shipping charges and could stand the excitement of meeting the mailman carrying a package.

Almost at the same time as my Sears Roebuck era, I became a radio fan. I had a Philco table radio shaped like the top of a cathedral door, and after ten in the evening the most wonderful jazz came on. I was enchanted by it. The clear bell-tone of a saxophone, played by a saxophonist using a hard reed, was especially great, as was the crisp sparkle of a piano. A female jazz vocalist who knew exactly where the real music was and could flat a note and fade into the exact key to make it jazzy and fine would delight me. I remember well the first night I ever heard "Stardust," probably some time in 1929, the year Hoagy Carmichael may have written the song. The next day I asked friends if they had heard it. It seemed to me such an unusual tune the first time I heard it. I wondered why it became popular only after many months of playing. Hoagy Carmichael was my kind of jazzman. Later, when I heard him sing, I also liked the gravelly, flatsy sort of timbre of his voice that was so perfect for his songs—"Georgia on My Mind," "Rockin' Chair," and "Buttermilk Sky."

Like many people, I tend to convert the sounds of music into visual experience, mainly colors. The sound of a trombone suggested to me a flow of molten copper changing direction as the notes change. Out of the bell of a french horn I could see a soft purple rope floating up and away into the air. A violin extruded a thin silver wire, sometimes with wool wrapped around it. Piccolos and flutes emitted floating bubbles of different colors. But the piano was best of all. A skilled artist playing one of Chopin's G-flat major etudes made showers of rhinestones cascade up out of the instrument, dazzling the whole area with brilliance.

Mum very much wanted me to learn to play the piano, but unfortunately at the time I started taking lessons, it was considered sissy for boys to play piano. I really regret not learning to play well, not only for the amount of money wasted on me, but simply because I have a deep love of music—all kinds—classical, jazz, country, and especially piano. I did learn to play a saxophone, but not very well. I really didn't care much about it, even though playing the saxophone was not considered sissy.

Meanwhile, Mum insisted it was essential that all of her sons go to dancing school. The Paris dancing school was held at Varden's Hall, in a big empty room two stories above Varden's Drug Store on Main Street. Some of the boys found it inconvenient to go to a toilet two floors down, so, since the second floor was unoccupied, we would go down one flight of stairs and find a far dark corner to relieve ourselves. This went on for some time. Then one day Mum got a call from Dr. Varden, the proprietor of the drugstore, saying all the plaster had fallen on his head in the back of the drugstore. His analysis of the problem convinced Mum, and I caught unshirted hell as a consequence.

But Mum's insistence that I go to dancing school paid off. I thought I was a good dancer. Joyland Park, just up the road toward Lexington, had all the big bands of the '20s and '30s—Fletcher Henderson, Coon-Sanders, Tal Henry, Clyde McCoy, Louis Armstrong, Duke Ellington. The dance hall was a big wooden barn. Twirling balls with little mirrors in them flashed colored lights across the floor. Very romantic. Joyland also had dance contests on occasion. A friend of mine, John Davis Haggard, won several of these contests. The prize was two dollars, one to each winner. Haggard was definitely a better dancer than I, but one night I was there with a particularly pretty young lady named Elisabeth "Lizo" Barbieux. We did rather well, I thought, but so did Haggard and his lady. We'd dance several numbers, and after each session we'd line up. As the spotlight fell on each couple, the other dancers would applaud. Each time the light came to us, I'd put my arm around Lizo and whisper to her, "Smile, Lizo, smile!" When she did, the applause was thunderous. We won the grand prize of two dollars. The victory was undoubtedly for Lizo's smile rather than my dancing. At least, I'm sure Haggard thought so.

FOUR

Horse Country

Bourbon is the only county I ever heard of that had a one-horse depression. I called it the "Tannery Panic." Edward Prichard Sr., father of my classmate Edward Prichard Jr. at Paris High School, owned a strapping big chestnut colt named Tannery, son of a sire named Ballot out of a mare named Blemished. He ran well as a two-year-old and won two important races in the Lexington Kentucky Association meet just before the Derby in the spring of 1930. Almost everybody in Bourbon County was a fan of his, and when he beat so many good horses in Lexington, people were near the point of remortgaging their farms and borrowing all the money they could to put it on his nose in the Derby. The *Kentuckian Citizen* said, "Prichard stands to win $62,000 in bets alone if Tannery wins the Derby." The writer saw only one horse as having a chance of beating Tannery, and that was Gallant Fox, winner of the Wood Memorial. Early in the winter Tannery was listed at 100 to 1 to win the Derby, and 25 to 1 to show. Prichard was said to have placed $500 on the horse to win and $500 to show.

The article further reported that a lot people were trying to buy part of Prichard's bets from him, but he wouldn't sell. Rumor had it that he declined an offer of $150,000 for Tannery and an agreement to divide his winnings 50-50 the rest of the season.

Derby day was Saturday, May 17, 1930. A few days earlier the New York stock market had had its heaviest trading day of the year, with 5,987,300 shares changing hands, some stocks down as much as sixteen points.

Edward George Villiers Stanley, the seventeenth Earl of Derby, was in Kentucky to present the winner's cup. Lord Derby was the house guest of Joseph E. Widener, the Philadelphia street railway tycoon, of whom one columnist said, "'Mr. Widener,' as his closest friends are pleased to call him, is just as plain as an old diamond tiara." Widener's spacious Elmendorf Farm was a few miles down the pike toward Lexington from the less impressive Ardery acres. A special train of the Louisville & Nashville railway carried Messrs. Widener and Stanley to Louisville on Derby day.

Tannery was pronounced fit by his trainer Jack Baker on Derby day, but so was the top favorite, Gallant Fox, who had been foaled in Bourbon County, son of A.B. Hancock's stallion Sir Gallahad III. The day was rainy and Tannery was known as a "good mudder." So far so good. After the playing of "My Old Kentucky Home" as the horses paraded to the starting gate, Bourbon County held its breath and listened to its radios.

The horses were off. Tannery laid about third until the half-mile pole but then began dropping back. About then Gallant Fox started his move on the back stretch, making the mile and a quarter in 2:07 and 3/5, less than record-breaking time but enough to win. A couple of weeks before, on April 30, Tannery had worked out a mile and an eighth in 1:54 and 3/5, and a *Courier-Journal* writer had said he "left little doubt that he would prove one of the most formidable of the western-owned hopes." But the Derby put him eighth, and Bourbon County suffered. Consequences of the Tannery Panic were felt in Paris for years. That day was far worse for many in the county than Black Tuesday, October 29, 1929, when the stock market crashed.

Racing and thoroughbred horses were part of Win's and my life, as they had to be for anybody in Bourbon County. Even though the Arderys didn't own any thoroughbreds, we loved the sport of racing. I well remember Saturday, May 6, 1933. It was another Derby day, and Win and I dressed in our Sunday best and got out on the road to race each other to Churchill Downs. The game was to see who could get to the Downs and steal his way into the clubhouse first—grandstand, of course, wasn't good enough.

Lots of cars on the road were headed for the track, and in those days a properly dressed boy had no trouble catching a ride. That day, as I recall, Win and I both climbed into a car that took us right to Churchill Downs. We asked to be let out on the back side of the track in the barn area. We climbed the fence and crossed the track to the back side of the infield and then walked to a spot just opposite the front of the clubhouse. We waited until about a dozen other youngsters were ready, and then all stormed the infield fence at once. There were guards swinging clubs, but we were too many for them. In a matter of seconds, we were both in the clubhouse in seats where we had an excellent view of the track. In those days there were clubhouse seats outside the box seat section.

That particular Derby was, to my mind, the most exciting one of all time. It was the famous race between Head Play and Broker's Tip. Coming down the stretch, about half a length ahead, was Mrs. Silas Mason's Head Play, jockey Herb Fisher in the irons. Driving up on the inside was Colonel E.R. Bradley's Broker's Tip, ridden by Don Meade. The way I saw it, Fisher sensed that another horse was closing up on him, halfway stood up in the saddle, and looked back. When that happened, Head Play seemed to break stride, and Broker's Tip came head to head with him.

There has since been much dispute about it, but it looked to me as if Fisher swung hard with his whip and hit Meade in the face. Meade then reached out and grabbed Head Play's bridle, and going to the wire there was a real tooth-and-nail fight between the jockeys. Broker's Tip was slightly ahead coming under the wire. Fisher claimed a foul, but it was disallowed, and Broker's Tip was declared the winner, giving Colonel Bradley his fourth Derby victory.

A Louisville *Courier-Journal* photographer who had rolled onto the track from the infield at the finish line took a most remarkable picture of the finish. Lying on his back and pointing his speedgraphic camera up, he snapped the picture and then rolled back under the rail as the horses thundered by. I consider it one of the greatest pictures of thoroughbred racing of all time.

Needless to say, Win and I, thumbing our way back to Bourbon County that evening, felt we had been greatly rewarded.

Head Play (left) and Broker's Tip heading for the finish line in the 1933 Kentucky Derby. Courtesy of the *Courier-Journal.*

My love of horses eventually helped me get my law degree. The Depression hit the Arderys pretty hard. In 1931, the year I graduated from Paris High School, I had between $250 and $300 in a savings and loan, money I had saved over the years from pay for odd jobs and various other sources. The savings account, as I recall, returned 4 percent. Good stocks were selling at rock bottom prices, and I decided that if the market went any lower the whole country would come apart. Nevertheless, I decided to buy stock. The man at the savings and loan said he thought I was crazy but wrote me out a check closing the account. Feeling very much the capitalist, as I recall, I bought a share or two of General Motors, also some DuPont, and General Electric.

When I went to the University of Kentucky, my parents paid my basic expenses, but I wanted some resources of my own. Eventually I found work at the university library that paid twenty-five cents an hour. Most of my work consisted of sitting by the door in the reserve reading room until the library closed in the evenings. I saved every penny I earned, and small bit by small bit invested it in the market. On the advice of an older friend, I bought a hundred shares of a stock called Swiss Oil that was selling over the counter at a dollar a share and paying a dividend of ten cents. A Kentuckian named Paul Blazer was running the company, which later changed its name to Ashland Oil. It went up.

Then one summer I got a job at Arlington Park Race Track in Chicago. The man who got me the job was Charley Kenney, Doc Kenney's son. Charley was a racehorse man and had some kind of executive job at Arlington. My job paid thirty-five cents an hour. I was a day laborer and did a variety of things—putting up the flag over the grandstand the morning of each racing day, working in a small infirmary or first-aid station with a doctor and a nurse during the day's races, and sweeping out the stands after the races were over. Those of us who swept out were called "stoopers." We swept up the literally thousands of tote tickets from the day's racing that littered the floor of the grandstand and clubhouse. A good stooper wrote the win, place, and show horses' numbers on a little card which he held in his hand at the top of the broom handle. By carefully eyeing the sweepings, a stooper could spot any winning ticket that might have been carelessly thrown away. Each day three or four such tickets were found by lucky stoopers, but stoop as I might, I never found one. One day the guy sweeping next to me picked up a fifty dollar bill. People get drunk and excited at race tracks and do careless things with their money and tote tickets.

I remember especially one day when I was in the infirmary just before the first race. A man came in and asked to speak to the doctor. He was a small-time horse owner who had a horse running that afternoon. Having forgotten the horse's name, I'll call him Saucy Boy.

It seemed the man owed a bill he hadn't been able to pay the doctor for some time. I heard most of the conversation, which was to the effect that Saucy Boy was sure to win the race and the owner would be in to pay the bill as soon as the race was over. This pleased the doctor, who appeared not to have any further interest in the matter. I engaged the guy in conversation and was told if I was smart I'd bet what I could on Saucy Boy to win. I asked the owner why he felt so sure. He said several things, one of which was that the horse was a good horse and the last three times out the owner wasn't trying to win with him. "Besides," he said, "today I got a jock that really knows how to ride him. You gotta give this horse a very special kind of a ride. If the jock gives him his head," he said, "he won't go. You gotta make him think he's running away with it. Then, he'll put his head down and really jump."

Foolishly, I didn't bet on the horse. But what the owner had said was so interesting that, when I heard the ringing of the bell and "They're off," I excused myself from duty with the doctor for a few minutes as though I were going to the john. I ran to the upper part of the grandstand and stood in an aisle where I could see the horses as they came out of the turn into the homestretch. As they came around the turn, the horses were fairly well bunched, and Saucy Boy was fifth or sixth. Then I could hardly believe my eyes. The jock reared back on him almost as though he was trying to pull him. Saucy Boy put his head down and really turned on the speed. He went wide coming around the pack and got under the wire a good two lengths ahead. The reins were still tight back from the bit, and I thought if that horse hadn't won, surely the judges would have set the jockey down for pulling him. It was almost a miracle, and one more example to convince me that horses are as different as people—maybe more so. Anyhow, the race was run just the way the owner said it would be, and the doc got paid. I kicked myself for not betting. I could have turned a two-dollar ticket into more than twenty dollars cash.

By the time the meet was over, I had saved every penny except for the expense of food at the workers' boarding room. I had a free bunk over the stables. As I departed, I paid two dollars to a horse van driver carrying three horses back to Lexington and climbed into an empty stall. I had slightly more than a hundred dollars in my pocket.

That hundred dollars, invested along with my savings and loan money and money from the library, resulted in my having just over $3,500 worth of stock when I went away to Harvard Law School. It was enough so that, with fifty dollars a month support from my parents and working during the summers, I was able to get my law degree three years later.

On December 7, 1941 (a date all people my age remember—the day the Japanese attacked Pearl Harbor), I was driving home from west Texas. I was a lieutenant in the Army Air Corps and a flying instructor at a Texas air base on leave. My beautiful Texas bride, Anne, was with me on her first trip to the Bluegrass. We'd gotten married the day before. When we heard about the Pearl Harbor attack, we knew it would be an unusual honeymoon. The next day, in Bourbon County, I was presented with a wire canceling my leave and ordering me back to military duty immediately. I determined to go AWOL for at least three days to let my wife meet my parents and friends. I also wanted to pay one special call. That was on two friends, Will Harbut and Man O' War (affectionately known as Big Red). To me they were the greatest show on earth, and I was determined that Anne should not return to Texas without having seen it.

December 9 was a beautiful winter day, as we drove up to the barn of Samuel D. Riddle's Faraway Farm, just outside Lexington. My friend Will Harbut was there to greet us, and although we were the only couple there that morning, he made us feel as though we were royalty. Will's face was just as I'd remembered it—wide and smiling, the color of seasoned walnut. He wore the same battered hat he had worn every time I ever saw him, turned down all around and looking like a gray felt bucket. His trousers were rumpled as though he and Big Red had slept in the same stall the night before. And his voice, when he spoke, was a rich, resonant baritone. There was something magical about Will, just as there was about Man O' War. In his presence you could feel it. He was a man of infinite kindness and courtesy coupled with strength.

I told Will about our truncated honeymoon. "I'm determined not to take my wife back to Texas without seeing one of the greatest

Phil and Anne Ardery in
1943, two years after
their marriage.

spectacles on earth," I said. He nodded. Anne looked at me as much
to say, "You're right. This man is something quite unusual."

Will put us through the routine of seeing other stallions in the
barn and then brought out Big Red. Man O' War stood beside the
old man, his gleaming head held high, his eyes blazing and ears
alert. He seemed enormous. I watched Anne catch her breath as
she took in his magnificence. He was truly like John Barrymore
making an entrance.

Then Will began to relate the things about him that I already
knew but longed to hear again. "Folks, this is Manna Waw. He the
greates hoss that evah lived. He the most and gonna go on bein' the
most long as you an' I can tell about it.

"He's foaled on Major Belmont's place ovah on the Georgetown
Pike. Mr. Riddles bought him for five thousan' dollahs. Some fella

Man O' War and his groom, Will Harbut. Courtesy of Keeneland
Library.

ask Mr. Riddles if he take a million dollahs for Manna Waw and he
say, 'Lotsa people got a million dollahs, I the onliest one got Manna
Waw.'"

Big Red occasionally would nuzzle Will as though he understood all this and approved. Will would say, "Stan' still, Red, these
folks wanna know all about yo' record.

"He's one of the greatest sires evah. He give us forty-seven stakes
winners."

Then Will would continue, "He stand sixteen an' a half hands
high. He weigh thirteen hunnert an' seventy fi pounds wid the longest stride o' any hoss on the track.

"On a fas' track he break a worl' record, on a slow track he win
by twenty lengths. He broke all records and broke down all the other
hosses."

There was a long pause. Then he said, "Onliest race he didn' win, the Jockey Club done set that jockey down an' he's been waukin' evah since." With this, an angry look would cloud Will's face. It was as though his own son had been cheated out of an inheritance. His hurt was real.

Then after a bit of small talk, Will turned to the champion. "Come on, Red. These folks got to go an' so do we." He gave a slight tug on the leather strap connected to the halter, and they both turned and walked back to the stall.

Over the years I've fitted as many facts into the Harbut epic as I could and found the old man guilty of very few inaccuracies. At first it seemed that Harbut was entirely wrong about jockey Johnny Loftus being "set down" for life for pulling Man O' War in his only loss—in the Sanford Memorial at Saratoga Springs in 1919. That race was won by a Harry Payne Whitney horse named Upset. It was a weird sort of race from many angles.

I had read that Samuel Riddle, Man O' War's owner, had allowed Loftus to ride Big Red three times after the Sanford Memorial in 1919. I mentioned this to Louisville turf writer Jim Bolus, a rock-solid authority. He said, "Yeah, but look at what happened to Loftus and Willie Knapp, Upset's rider, the next year. They both were refused licenses and in fact were left 'walking ever since.'" Both regained esteem in the minds of most race goers, and both ultimately wound up in Saratoga's National Museum of Racing Hall of Fame.

But the 1919 Sanford Memorial was indeed an odd race. Racing historians have pretty well spelled out many of the details of that contest. Upset and Man O' War had met before. In fact, they met six times other than at the Sanford Memorial, and Man O' War won all six of the other races, usually carrying heavier weight than Upset. He carried fifteen pounds more than Upset in the Sanford.

Upset was a good horse, the runner-up in both the Kentucky Derby and the Preakness. Owner Whitney and trainer Jim Rowe refused to give up against the red giant; indeed, sixteen of the starters against Man O' War were Whitney horses.

Racegoers the day of the Sanford Memorial evidently thought the best chance against Riddle's champion was a horse named

Golden Broom, who had been bought at the same Saratoga auction as Man O' War and brought more than three times the price Riddle paid for Big Red.

The regular starter, Mars Cassidy, did not appear at the Saratoga track the day of the Sanford Memorial. Why he didn't has never been clear. At any rate, the substitute starter was Charles H. Pettingill, a man in his seventies who had had several bad starts that day. Some said he "couldn't see across the race track."

All reports indicate that Man O' War got a very bad start. Apparently he was obstreperous, breaking through the old-fashioned web barrier several times. Pettingill warned Loftus to keep Man O' War lined up but then sent the horses on their way while Loftus and his mount were moving back. Loftus later said he had been instructed to lay back until Golden Broom tired a bit, so he went to the rail behind Golden Broom and Upset. Coming into the stretch, Golden Broom began to tire. At this point, Man O' War was pocketed, and Loftus tried to find room to go through on the rail, but Upset had him blocked. This left Loftus no choice but to go outside.

It was only the lack of another jump or two that kept Man O' War from keeping his perfect record. Jockey Knapp later said, "There wasn't no doubt who was the best horse in the race," and added, "Sometimes I'm sorry I didn't do it," meaning he might have let Man O' War come through. But Knapp was also quoted as saying that "a boy who let a horse through on the rail never got a second chance with the same trainer."

After the race, rumors abounded among the fans. One was that Loftus and Knapp had made a large bet at long odds on Upset. But as the clamor died down, most racing cognoscenti believed the outcome was the result of an odd combination of circumstances, part and parcel of racing. When the Jockey Club refused licenses to the two jockeys the next year, no reasons were given. It was thought that a cloud still hung over the Sanford Memorial of the year before.

I recently asked Tom Harbut, Will's son, what he thought in light of his father's comment. Tom's response was, "Who knows what happened? There was no television coverage of the race, as there would be today. That, if it had been available, might well have told the story. But even today we have unsolved mysteries. And so Will Harbut was essentially correct in saying the Jockey Club put Loftus down and left him walking the rest of his days.

In May 1946 my friend Will Harbut suffered a stroke that took his eyesight and left him paralyzed on the right side. He never recovered and died the next year. Less than a month after his death, on November 1, 1947, Man O' War died in his stall at Faraway Farm. No doubt grief from the loss of his worshipful companion hastened Big Red's demise.

FIVE

✢

Ed Simms and Xalapa

Billionaire? What does it take to make a billionaire? How does he count his money? The answer is, he doesn't. He doesn't know the extent of his wealth at any moment, any more than Texan Nelson Bunker Hunt did a few years ago when his corner of the silver market broke off.

Kentuckian Edward Francis Simms, born in Paris, Bourbon County, March 5, 1870, from time to time was clearly in that class. Simms hit it big when oil was struck at Spindletop, near Beaumont, Texas, shortly after the turn of the century. He was one of the first to exploit the sulphur domes near New Orleans in 1910, using the Frasch process to bring sulphur out of the ground in liquid form. He organized the Freeport Sulphur Company, the first sulphur royalty company in the United States. He produced over five million tons of sulphur at the Texas Bryan Mound alone.

Based in Houston in 1916, Simms brought in two wells in nearby Goose Creek oil field, Sweet Well No. 1, with an initial production of 30,000 barrels a day and another, Sweet Well No. 16, with initial production of 18,000 barrels a day. Those two alone, among his many wells in the Goose Creek field, at a price of $17 a barrel would have yielded revenue of more than $800,000 a day.

On December 27, 1924, the *Kentuckian-Citizen* reported that "Simms is a large owner of real estate . . . He owns a fee simple 1,800,000 acres of land in Old Mexico, 1,250,000 acres in oil leases in Louisiana and other land. . . . He reported also he owned 2,800 acres in Kentucky."

Although he always proclaimed himself a Bourbon County Ken-

Ed Simms (left) with James W. McClelland. Courtesy of Keeneland Library, Cook Collection.

tuckian, locally Simms was known mainly because of his farm outside Paris, called Xalapa. He was also locally famous because of his rich man/poor man ups and downs, which drastically affected the economy of the whole county.

His father, also a Bourbon Countian, was a man of wealth but not enormous wealth. He educated his sons well. Ed and his brother, Will, both graduated from Yale in 1891, and his father named a thoroughbred racer "Yale 91" in honor of the event. Sports pages reported that "Yale 91" won a fast race at Chicago, "defeating a good field of horses."

Young Ed, not satisfied with an engineering degree from Yale, went on to get a law degree from the University of Virginia three years later. In later years he had the advantage over many other oil field traders, who were amazed at his knowledge of contracts and leases as well as oil field engineering.

Ed's father was William Emmett Simms, and his mother, Lucy Ann (Blythe) Simms from Madison County, Kentucky. As a young man, William was a promising lawyer who received his law degree with honors from Transylvania in 1845 and began practice in Paris. Before the War between the States, William Simms served as a member of the U.S. Congress. Later he served as a Confederate colonel, First Battalion, Kentucky Cavalry, and still later as a senator in the Confederate Congress and a member of the cabinet of President Jefferson Davis. The old Colonel died on his Bourbon County estate in 1898, leaving a considerable fortune to his sons, Will and Ed, and his daughter, Lucy.

Ed ran through his inheritance fast and took off for Texas. Bourbon Countians believed Ed would surely come back one day to beg a crust of bread from Will. But that wasn't what happened. He wildcatted for oil in Texas and Mexico—no one seems to know where he got his first stake—and came back to Bourbon County with many times the wealth he had before leaving. That was when he began buying Bluegrass farmland and adding to what was to become the idyllically beautiful Xalapa Farm, named for a little town in Mexico. The name, a Mexican-Indian word, is pronounced Ha-lá-pa.

The 2,800 acres of Xalapa lay eight miles east of Paris. As a child, I had the run of the farm because of the friendship between my father and the farm manager. Most of the farm was surrounded by a high stone wall. There was an imposing water tower, also built of native limestone, on the highest point of land with a large ship's bell that rang beautifully from time to time. Stoner Creek, broad as many rivers, ran through the farm and there was a dam to make it wide and grand. Beside the dam was a restored water mill cooling its feet in the quiet, beautiful stream.

Two large lakes on the farm were stocked with fish supplied by the farm's own fish hatchery. A swimming pool was made to look like a natural part of the landscape, and what served as a diving board was a large rock overhanging a wall of limestone boulders. There is no telling how many times as a boy I jumped off that rock into the delicious waters below. Running from what looked like a natural, flowing spring was a brook that kept the pool filled.

Behind the swimming pool was a lovely path winding through a woodland from which a stroller could see half-hidden little stone elves, one pouring out a flagon of wine, one netting a butterfly, and others doing things elves do. The elves, it was said, came from the Black Forest of Germany.

Simms brought workers from Mexico to build some fifteen miles of macadam roads and bridges, work on the tall stone wall around the farm, and generally beautify the pasturelands and woodlands. He had at one time more than a hundred Mexicans at work. Much of this work was done under the supervision of an English gardener.

Simms had his own rock quarry and from it hewed material for a stone horse barn with a quarter-mile exercise track inside so his thoroughbreds could be exercised on rainy days without getting wet. There have been exercise tracks something like that elsewhere, but Simms possibly had the first and certainly the most elaborate one.

Many years before the Keeneland yearling sales at Lexington began, Simms loaded his horses at the Paris rail depot for shipment to Saratoga. Because there were no horse vans at that time, grooms and stable boys would walk the yearlings some eight miles from the farm to the Paris depot. I was nearly always there for the event, and I remember seeing him—straw boater on his head, undershirt but no shirt, galluses holding up his pants—sitting in the front seat of a Locomobile town car with a neatly liveried black chauffeur sitting beside him. (The enormous Locomobile was the car General Pershing had used as his personal staff car during World War I. It was the American Rolls Royce of its day.) The fractious yearlings would tug at their halters as young black men tried to get them to walk up the ramp and into the box cars. Usually it was necessary for two to grab the halter and two more to lock arms behind a colt to get it in the car and into a stall.

James W. McClelland was a Lexingtonian and a boyhood friend

The stone horse barn at Xalapa. Courtesy of the *Courier-Journal*.

to whom Simms, for a time, trusted all his beloved thoroughbreds. The year 1920 was great for the Simms-McClelland combination. That year, on McClelland's advice, Simms bought the entire yearling crop of America's premier thoroughbred breeder, August Belmont. The crop included My Play, a full brother of Man o' War. That was also the year he imported Prince Palatine, sire of Prince Pal, from England, and paid the second highest price ever paid by an American for a foreign horse.

In late 1929 the bottom fell out of the Simms empire, and Simms simply disappeared. A story making the rounds in Paris was that he flew out of Xalapa in a Ford Trimotor airplane. No one really knew how he departed or where he went. The farm was left with those who lived on it. The farm manager was gone, and the farm was like a pilotless ship. The tenants cropped the farm, mostly in tobacco, and pocketed the proceeds. After several years passed and no one

The Tudor-style tower at Xalapa. Courtesy of the *Courier-Journal.*

had seen hide nor hair of the master, the *Kentuckian-Citizen* on September 3, 1937, published a story about the Simms Petroleum Company being sold: "Edward F. Simms of Bourbon has completed a deal for the sale of his oil lands and mineral holdings in Louisiana at the reported price of $26 million. These holdings are reported to be among the most valuable in the entire South."

That story produced a motorcade of grocerymen, lumberyard

owners, hardware storekeepers, and the like, all headed out from Paris to Xalapa. It turned out that Simms had returned to Xalapa unannounced and was living in a hut beside the high stone wall. Again he was rich, though not as rich as he had been. Everybody got paid. One groceryman was said to have collected more than $12,000—a lot of groceries in those days. Once again the flag flew over the water tower with the ship's bell, the pool was filled, and fish were happily hatching in the fish hatchery. To Bourbon Countians, this seemed the most fabulous event of its kind in history.

During the summer of 1937, I was working as a clerk in a Wall Street law firm. One of our wealthy clients invited me to the races at Saratoga. It happened that our box was adjacent to the box of Mr. Sam Riddle, owner of Man o' War. I was introduced to Riddle as a young man from Bourbon County, Kentucky.

Immediately Mr. Riddle took off, telling me some of his recollections of our old neighbor, Ed Simms. He said that a number of years earlier he was sitting in his box at Saratoga carefully watching the goings on between Simms and the Whitneys, both in nearby boxes. Apparently both had horses in the upcoming race, and they were betting against each other. The betting on each side went to more than $100,000, and neither horse ran in the money. Riddle said Simms didn't bat an eye. He concluded: "They tell you about Diamond Jim Brady and Bet-a-Million Gates, but I don't think there ever was anybody that could hold a candle to Simms."

Ed Simms died of leukemia in Johns Hopkins Hospital, Baltimore, on December 6, 1938, at the age of sixty-eight. He was first buried in the Paris cemetery, but his body was later removed to Houston, Texas. At the time of his death, Xalapa farm and the Simms fortune were in one of many stages of recovery. The farm then was home to sixty-five broodmares, twenty-five yearlings, and twenty-eight foals as well as a fine horse named Xalapa Clown. Xalapa Clown, unbeaten as a two-year-old, was a son of Eternal, a great Simms sire of earlier years who was the champion two-year-old of 1918 but lost the Kentucky Derby to his great rival, Sir Barton, in 1919.

Until her recent death, Mrs. P. Whitney Webb, the granddaughter of Simms's widow, lived on the farm and carried on his tradition as an outstanding breeder of thoroughbreds. Under her own name, Lillie F. Webb, she sold at Keeneland in the fall of 1982 six of her yearlings for $357,200. This was only $49,800 less than Simms got for his entire stock in 1924. She was selling in the magic shadow of the Bourbon County billionaire.

SIX

Claiborne Farm

Sometimes the frame of a picture is so interesting that we study it before we really look at the picture in it. The story of Claiborne Farm—a farm that likely has produced more stakes-winning thoroughbred horses than any similar establishment in the history of racing—is framed in the history of Bourbon County.

"By 1838," writes Kentucky historian Thomas D. Clark, "the fertile county of Bourbon, reporting a negligible production of grain and tobacco, led the list in livestock . . . with 10,000 head of cattle, 40,000 hogs, 3,000 horses and mules." Bourbon County historian H.E. Everman, discussing sheep raising, says that Bourbon citizen "Graybeard" Sam Clay about that same time "raised the largest flock of Southdowns, some 8,000."

This Sam Clay's long gray beard helped citizens of the Bluegrass distinguish him from his distant Clay cousins "Mule Sam" and "Whiskey Sam." When "Graybeard" died, he left nearly 14,000 acres of choice land, much of it in Bourbon County. His granddaughter Nancy Clay married Arthur B. Hancock Sr. of Virginia, and part of the Bourbon County acres ultimately became Claiborne Farm.

Most people have one or two days in the past they remember vividly. For me the day of the attack on Pearl Harbor was one of those days. I can remember everything about that day—what I had on, what I ate, what I did.

Such a day for the Hancocks of Claiborne Farm was Saturday, May 5, 1984. That was the day Swale, more of a family pet than a thoroughbred racehorse, thundered down the stretch at Churchill Downs in Louisville for an easy three-and-a-quarter length vic-

Swale winning the 1984 Belmont Stakes. Photo by Bob Coglianese, courtesy of *The Blood-Horse.*

tory in the hundred and tenth running of the Kentucky Derby.

Swale had been beaten in the Lexington Stakes at Keeneland two weeks before, and the railbirds had it that he was training poorly and might even be scratched. But nobody told Swale that, and he managed to cover the Derby's mile and a quarter in a winning 2:02 2/5. Jockey Laffit Pincay Jr., following the wise guidance of veteran trainer Woody Stephens, had him in good position, running smoothly down the backstretch with the favorite, the filly Althea, hanging onto a slim lead. Swale passed Althea at the three-eighths pole, and from then on the running was easy.

Seth Hancock, president of the Claiborne Farm organization, had taken over after the death of his father, A.B. Hancock Jr., generally known as "Bull." That was in 1972. Seth, Bull's third of four children, was twenty-four at the time, and his youth scared some of the thoroughbred breeders associated with the farm. But Seth soon showed that he had breeding in his blood. He had it from three generations back, when his great-grandfather, Captain Richard

Hancock, a veteran of Lee's Army of Northern Virginia, became a breeder of thoroughbreds.

Swale's 1984 Derby victory was special for the Hancocks in many ways. It had been Bull Hancock's unfulfilled ambition all of his life to breed and run a Derby winner in the golden silks of Claiborne Farm. The farm had bred many top stakes winners, including the only father-son Triple Crown winners, Gallant Fox and Omaha. But they raced for other owners—the Woodwards, the Phippses, the Mellons.

When Swale's dam, Tuerta, was foaled, Bull Hancock was bitterly disappointed. He had wanted a colt and he got a filly. Not only that, Tuerta had only one eye. Even so, she won her first stakes race at two, giving Bull a final major victory before his death. According to Seth, "That had a lot to do with our decision to keep her."

Swale, the leggy, dark bay Seattle Slew-Tuerta colt, was picked by Seth's mother, Waddell Hancock, as part of an agreement with Raceland Stable. The stable is a partnership that includes Peter Brant, Ed Cox, William Haggin Perry, and the Hancocks (Waddell, daughters Dell and Clay, and son Seth). Waddell says, "I had the fifth choice that year. I just sort of had a hunch that this was the colt that could do it."

The Hancocks' special feeling about Swale showed in the particular tenderness with which he was raised. Swale would fall fast asleep, snoring loudly, in his stall and never move a muscle when Dell Hancock would come in and lie down with her head on his neck. He was in fact like a house pet. There was also the fact that Dell's older brother Arthur, owner of nearby Stone Farm, had already taken the Derby in 1982 with his Gato del Sol. So Swale had to do the same for Claiborne.

After Swale's Derby victory, Seth Hancock had doubts about trying for the Preakness, but he said, "After he won the Derby so easily, you had to try it." Swale had a bad day and lost the Preakness, finishing seventh. Seth was "disappointed, but I was not surprised." Nevertheless, he sent Swale on to the Belmont, the last and longest of the Triple Crown races.

A week before the Belmont, Eddie Maple, working with trainer Woody Stephens, sent Swale at a reasonable pace through seven furlongs; then, the day before the race, he blew the colt out over a half-mile at :48 3/5. The pre-Belmont preparation was just what Woody wanted.

The greatest test of all came June 9, 1984, at the Belmont. Swale was first choice for the crowd despite his poor Preakness run. Second choice was Play On, the place horse of the Preakness, and Preakness winner Gate Dancer was third. Jockey Laffit Pincay Jr. had Swale in good enough shape to take the lead going into the first turn. From then on Pincay held his advantage, making the other horses play his game. The first six furlongs Swale covered in an unspectacular 1:13 3/5, but he did the second six in exactly the same and went on to win by four lengths. He had run the mile-and-a-half as fast as any previous winner save three. Thus Swale became the superstar of racing, with bright prospects for the Breeders' Cup in November.

But tragedy sometimes strikes with great suddenness when fragile thoroughbreds are involved. Nine days after his stunning Belmont victory, Swale was dead. He had returned from a light gallop, apparently in excellent condition. A few moments later in the yard outside trainer Woody Stephens's barn, his hind legs went down under him, and he never got up again. An autopsy was performed, but no explanation was ever given.

The Hancocks' heartbreak was indescribable. Grief hung like a pall over the entire farm as an oak casket lined with farm colors and carrying the body of the champion was lowered into a grave behind the farm office.

Most people in the thoroughbred horse business think of Claiborne Farm in Kentucky as part and parcel of the Hancock family—the late Bull Hancock, his wife, Waddell, and their children. Seth Hancock, Bull's son, is now president of Claiborne. Seth knows how much of Claiborne's present belongs to its past. There can be little doubt that the ghost of Captain Richard Hancock keeps careful watch over Claiborne Farm, sees the breeding, foaling, breaking, and all other major events, and whispers from time to time in his great-grandson's ear about just which "nicks" of the various bloodlines will work best.

Richard Hancock, three times wounded, was on his way to General Lee's headquarters for reassignment and further duty on April 9, 1865. That afternoon he was on the outskirts of Lynchburg when he received word of the surrender at Appomattox. His first thoughts were of his bride, the former Thomasia Overton Harris of Ellerslie near Charlottesville, whom he had married during a period of recovery only five months earlier; so he returned to his once beautiful Ellerslie, now desolated by war but home to him and his young wife.

Captain Hancock, now in charge of Ellerslie, soon began rebuilding the thoroughbred stock begun before the war by his bride's father. The next years were busy ones at Ellerslie, especially for Thomasia, who on June 25, 1875, presented the Captain with his fifth child, a boy to be named Arthur Boyd Hancock. As it happened, that was the year of the first running of the Kentucky Derby. Also about that time, Ellerslie acquired a beautiful blooded stallion named Scathelock. By imported Eclipse, out of Fanny Washington, Scathelock was bred and raised by Major Thomas W. Doswell on his farm, Bullfield, near Richmond.

With the acquisition of Scathelock, Ellerslie launched its reputation as one of the finest breeding establishments in the country. The next thoroughbred mare Captain Hancock was able to buy was War Song by War Dance. She was from Kentucky stock. One of her foals was a colt named Blenheim. By an odd coincidence, that name cropped up again many years later when the Captain's son, Arthur B. Hancock, imported the English stallion, Blenheim II, who played an important part in the success of Claiborne Farm in Kentucky.

At the time Captain Hancock acquired Scathelock, he did his best to get Major Doswell to part with a half brother of Scathelock, a stallion named Eolus. The Major declined. But some years later, after Eolus had changed hands several times, Hancock managed to acquire him. Eolus did well at Ellerslie; at the Preakness in the spring of 1886, three of the five horses in the race were by Eolus. That

Preakness was the first major race ever attended by Arthur Hancock, then eleven years old.

Young Arthur grew and prospered. He first entered Johns Hopkins University and later switched to the University of Chicago, where he received his A.B. degree in the summer of 1895. He was a very good if not outstanding scholar, especially in mathematics. But scholarship was not his cup of tea; he decided to stay with the farm. The first year of young Arthur's return to Ellerslie found him a mere wage-earner looking after the mares, foals, and yearlings and serving as a general helper in management of the farm. The next year Arthur became a partner.

Captain Hancock had developed a practice of selling most of the yearling produce of Ellerslie, some at Pimlico but most in New York. His policy was to keep many of the fillies. By this time the progeny of Eolus, by imported Leamington-Fanny Washington, was doing extremely well and contributing to the growing reputation of Ellerslie. A partnership with Bullfield, the Doswells' place near Richmond, was an additional source of strength and prestige. Major Doswell died in 1890, and the Bullfield operation was taken over by his son.

Though the business at Ellerslie was reasonably prosperous, the price of its yearlings was pathetic. Throughout America there was a wave of piety; popular disapproval of racetrack betting would peak in 1908, when it was outlawed in New York, which had been the center of the racing industry and of the American market for thoroughbreds. Kentucky and Maryland were left as the main supports for the "Sport of Kings." Some of the more prominent stables folded. But the Hancocks weathered the storm.

Arthur had made numerous trips to the New York yearling auctions, and on one such occasion met Johnson N. Camden of Woodford County, Kentucky, who was, among other things, an official of the Bluegrass Fair in Lexington. Camden was evidently impressed with young Hancock and invited him to judge a horse show at the forthcoming Bluegrass Fair of 1907. In the course of his Kentucky visit, Hancock accepted an invitation from another prominent Kentuckian, Catesby Woodford. On that visit he met Miss

Nancy Clay of Marchmont, one of the loveliest places in all central Kentucky.

When the law prohibiting gambling at racetracks in New York went into effect, the Hancocks, father and son, decided not to attempt to sell any yearlings at the regular Fasig-Tipton sale at Sheepshead Bay, Long Island. But for all the tales of adversity in the horse business, there was little letup in the courtship of Mr. Hancock of Virginia and Miss Clay of Kentucky. The affair progressed excitedly to the fateful day of June 30, 1908, when the two were married at her parents' home outside Paris, Kentucky.

The newlyweds returned to Ellerslie and set themselves to the task of renovating an old house on a tract of land adjoining the main farm. But the ties to Kentucky were strong, made stronger by upcoming events. Arthur and Nancy Hancock were visiting her parents in Kentucky when, on January 24, 1910, at Marchmont, Nancy gave birth to their first child and named him Arthur Boyd Hancock Jr. Hastening events still further was the death of Nancy's parents within a few days of each other shortly after midyear.

In the division of the extensive Clay lands, Nancy inherited about 1,300 acres of "the best land in Bourbon County," on which her grandfather, Graybeard Sam, had raised Southdowns in the previous century. Logic would dictate that Arthur Hancock, with his years of experience, would manage that property. Captain Richard Hancock had died in 1912 after a short retirement. Ellerslie was now well managed and in good hands, but the Bourbon County property had to have the kind of attention Arthur Hancock was prepared to provide. So in 1915 the Hancocks moved to Paris.

At the time, a friend had just given up the name of his Bluegrass establishment, "Claiborne," to give it another name. Nancy Hancock liked the name, perhaps because it had a local history and also had within it the sound of her maiden name. Accordingly, the new place was named Claiborne.

Eolus had made Ellerslie widely recognized as an outstanding breeding establishment. His colt, Eole, at the ages of four and five was ranked as the best stallion in America. But now Eolus was gone, and Hancock looked for another outstanding stallion to keep his hold on success. He found that stallion in Celt, owned by James R. Keene of Lexington. Celt had a good, though not outstanding, record on the track; but, as a son of Commando, he had a bloodline that appealed to Hancock. Keene wouldn't sell the stallion but did lease him to Hancock for two years. When the lease ran out in 1912, no renewal was granted, and Celt returned to Keene's Castleton Stud. Keene, however, died that same year, and Hancock bought Celt in a dispersal sale for $25,000.

Celt became America's leading sire in 1919, and as the breeding operation progressed at both Ellerslie in Virginia and Claiborne in Kentucky, Hancock renewed his quest for outstanding stallions. He made contact for the first time with the British Bloodstock Agency. Of those offered by the agency, Hancock liked the looks of one named Wrack. He bought Wrack for a modest $8,000 and stood him at Claiborne. Wrack soon rose to the top of America's leading sires and stayed there for more than a decade.

Hancock had made a sufficient name for himself to draw around him other big names in the racing business. One of these was William Woodward, successor to August Belmont II as chairman of the Jockey Club. Woodward was head of New York's Hanover Bank. As a businessman interested in racing, he was happy to give much of his horse business to Claiborne Farm, transferring his weanlings to his lush 2,500-acre Blair Stud near Bowie, Maryland.

At Hancock's request, William Woodward joined Marshall Field and Robert Fairbairn to buy the great stallion Sir Gallahad III (Teddy–Plucky Leige) in 1926. Sir Gallahad's first crop at Claiborne produced the 1930 Triple Crown winner Gallant Fox, the only Triple Crown winner to produce another Triple Crown winner, Omaha. Hancock formed another syndicate that in 1936 bought Blenheim II from the Aga Khan. Blenheim was made famous by being the sire from his first season of another Triple Crown winner, Whirlaway. The highly successful breeding of thoroughbreds continued at both Ellerslie and Claiborne until 1946, when Hancock sold Ellerslie and transferred all his stock to Claiborne.

Success after success followed Arthur Hancock Sr. in his operation of Claiborne. His honesty and sober way of going about breeding thoroughbreds, a business that throughout history has had its charlatans and fakirs, drew many prominent names to him. He was a tall, fine-looking man, something of the J.P. Morgan type, as I remember him.

For all his seriousness, he had a strong place in the hearts of nearly all who knew him, certainly of those closest to him, the ones who worked for him. The Claiborne resident veterinarian in a 1977 speech to the Paris Rotary Club said, "My association with Mr. Hancock Sr. was the greatest and nicest thing that ever happened to me."

Arthur Hancock Sr. suffered a stroke in 1947 from which he never completely recovered. But the saga of Claiborne was to continue when son Bull Hancock took over. Arthur Jr. got the nickname "Bull" as a prep-school football player, and it stuck with him throughout life.

Bull Hancock married a Nashville beauty named Waddell Walker in 1941. By that time he had been made foreman of all the horses at Claiborne and was well established in the management of the farm. His bride was the daughter of Seth Walker, a prominent member of the Tennessee bar and a distinguished trial attorney. Bull and Waddell met, naturally, at the Keeneland Races in Lexington. That same year they had watched the thrilling 1939 Kentucky Derby victory of Claiborne-bred Johnstown, owned by William Woodward.

When Bull assumed command of the Claiborne establishment after a stint in the Army Air Corps during World War II, he set out to change things a little. He held back a few fillies each year, ones that might have been sent to the sales. He sold the great sire Round Table but retained a quarter interest in him. And later he evolved a scheme to sell half-interest in all his stock. William Haggin Perry was the main partner in Bull's new venture. The farm's success was built largely on such sires as Bold Ruler and the imported Princequillo and Nasrullah. Bull thought the Round Table–Nasrullah cross a particularly good nick. And Bold Ruler led the sire list eight times, including among his progeny the great Secretariat, who broke

Claiborne Farm. Photo by Dell Hancock.

many records and in 1973 became the first Triple Crown winner in twenty-five years. Many thoroughbred experts say his Belmont record-breaking victory by thirty-one lengths stands as the greatest mile and a half ever run by a racehorse.

The sires Bull Hancock had standing at Claiborne led all the sires in the United States seventeen times during the years 1955 through 1973. Bull died in 1972 while on a hunting trip in Scotland. He had taken much from his forebears and had added his own twist. In 1954 he had changed his father's pattern of selling the entire output of yearlings and made it a practice to train and race some of the best ones, many of them under the arrangement he had established with his partner, William Haggin Perry.

Bull's oldest son, A.B. Hancock III, soon after his father's death, elected to establish his own operation nearby at a location bearing the well known name Stone Farm. This left the younger brother, Seth, a twenty-four-year-old at the time, to take charge at Claiborne.

Seth, a tall, blue-eyed, candid young man, soon gained the confidence of the many prominent horsemen who had dealt with the Claiborne operation for years.

Seth Hancock has earned a reputation for his no-nonsense, old-fashioned style as a horse breeder. Many "bluegrass" horse breeders have turned to Kentucky fescue, a bluegrass look-alike, which they think makes a hardier sod than bluegrass. Not Seth. The grass at Claiborne is the old-style Kentucky bluegrass with just a little native clover mixed in.

His philosophy of breeding horses as he told it to me, is simply, "Breed the best to the best and expect the best." Bloodlines mean nearly everything but you have to understand which "nicks" seem to join which bloodlines for optimum results. Seth was born knowing lots about the magic of "nicks."

I once mentioned to Seth that some thoroughbred breeders allowed the queen of England free access to their farms to board her broodmares and free seasons to their best stallions. His response was, "If the queen wishes to do business with Claiborne, it will be on the same basis as anyone else."

When Queen Elizabeth II visited Woodford County breeder William Farish in October 1984, she expressed a desire to see the Claiborne Farm operation. Farish called Waddell Hancock and arranged a visit. When Waddell told her son Seth the queen was coming, his reply was, "Mother, you got us into this, now you take care of it." His mother responded, "Seth, ordinarily I don't lay down the law around here, but this time the law is that the queen is coming and you're going to show her around."

Seth found himself seated at lunch beside Her Majesty. When I asked him about the luncheon conversation, he remarked somewhat brusquely, "It's pretty hard to talk to someone when you can't ask a question." But the queen had her tour of the farm and accepted the invitation to feed a handful of mints to the retired veteran Round Table when she visited his barn. Whether she has ever sought to do business with Claiborne, I cannot say, but I feel sure that if she did she would be dealt with "on the same basis as anyone else."

The years of Seth Hancock's management have produced two Eclipse awards as the nation's outstanding breeder. They have also produced the great Swale, the first Kentucky Derby winner ever to carry the golden silks of Claiborne Farm. Recently Claiborne has been home to such top stallions as Mr. Prospector, Nijinsky II, Danzig, Secretariat, Spectacular Bid, Damascus, and many others.

The flag over Claiborne Farm has never flown quite as high as it flies today. In fact, in the very early morning, if you stand in any pasture of the farm and listen carefully, you may be able to hear Captain Richard Hancock of Lee's Army of Northern Virginia let out a Rebel cheer.

SEVEN

A Hero of World War I

In the summer of 1940, Howard Henderson, a hard-punching, cold-blooded political reporter for the Louisville *Courier-Journal*, commenting on my having just volunteered for pilot training in the U.S. Army Air Corps, said to me, "Phil, I think a war's coming, as you apparently do. I was in the Paris Cemetery the other day and noted what a beautiful place it is and particularly the grave of Reuben Hutchcraft."

My father had often pointed out Hutchcraft's grave to me, saying, "Here lies perhaps Bourbon County's greatest hero of World War I." Henderson continued, "Hutchcraft was a Bourbon County graduate of Harvard Law School like you, and I've got you picked as the Reuben Hutchcraft of World War II." I made no reply. I hoped to be luckier than Hutchcraft and come back alive from the war. One day after I got home from the war, I saw Howard on the street, and he said, "Phil, I'm sorry I made that comment to you about Reuben Hutchcraft." Howard was a mean reporter, and that was the only time I ever heard him apologize to anyone.

Reuben Hutchcraft's roots were deeper in the soil than most. His great grandfather, Thomas Hutchcraft, was a drummer boy in the American Revolution. One of his mother's ancestors was a sister of Daniel Boone and was one of the heroic women who carried water to the besieged at Bryan's Station while it was under Indian attack in 1782.

Hutchcraft was college valedictorian and top honors student at Transylvania College in Lexington in 1907. Later he was a Harvard law student and an associate editor of the *Harvard Law Review* and graduated with top honors in 1911. Then he served as a two-term member of the Kentucky General Assembly, a leader in the commission that revised Kentucky's tax laws, a professor of law at the University of Kentucky, a Sunday school teacher at the Paris Christian Church, and, last, a volunteer in the service of his country in the "war to end all wars."

Thursday, June 13, 1907, was a bright day for young Reuben Brent Hutchcraft. He and his sister Mary Fithian Hutchcraft were receiving Bachelor of Arts degrees from Transylvania's College of Liberal Arts. Reuben was president of the graduating class and delivered the salutatory address, an oration later commended in the press as outstanding "for elegance of diction, clearness of thought and the embellishments that characterize an impressive and dramatic oratorical effect." For a young man who had not yet reached his twenty-first birthday this was certainly a glorious beginning. Although it was reported that he was expected to enter the "law department" of the University of Virginia, he in fact went to Harvard Law School.

At Harvard his leadership qualities were immediately recognized. Among the many close friends he met there was a student named Henry Breckinridge of Lexington, who was later to become a colonel in the army, an Olympic fencing star, and an attorney for Charles A. Lindbergh. Colonel Breckinridge reminisced in a letter to a friend written after Hutchcraft's death about how "for two years we sat together at the same table in Memorial Hall while attending the Harvard Law School."

Ever the Kentucky politician and an ardent Democrat, Hutchcraft won a hotly contested election for president of the Democratic Club of Harvard in the spring of 1910. His election was an overwhelming defeat for his opponent because it had become enmeshed in an earlier Boston municipal election in which Hutchcraft had opposed the powerful forces of John "Honey Fitz" Fitzgerald, local Irish boss and maternal grandfather of President-to-be John F. Kennedy.

In the Harvard Democratic Club election, anti-Irish cards were distributed in an effort to create a backlash against Hutchcraft. But after it was revealed that the cards were circulated by a supporter

Reuben Hutchcraft. Courtesy
of Transylvania University
Library.

of Hutchcraft's opponent, the backlash went in the opposite direction, giving Reuben a landslide victory.

Hutchcraft was prominent not only as a young politician from
Kentucky but also as a legal scholar. He was elected associate editor of the *Harvard Law Review* when Robert T. Swaine was president of the *Review*. Swaine later founded a prestigious Wall Street
law firm, now Cravath, Swaine and Moore, one of the great inter-
national firms, with offices in New York and London.

But Hutchcraft was always a Kentuckian. Upon graduation from
law school and passage of the bar exam, he made his home in Paris.
There he associated himself with an established local attorney, David
Cline, in offices on the second floor of the Kentuckian-Citizen Newspaper Building on Bank Row. It was noted in the *Kentuckian-Citizen* of July 8, 1911, that he, with other representatives of the local
bar, attended a meeting of the State Bar Association in Lexington
where they heard Governor Woodrow Wilson of New Jersey de-
liver the principal address.

The young Harvard lawyer lost little time in becoming involved in local politics. In early May 1913, he announced his candidacy for state representative. The local press commented: "He is a wide-awake and popular gentleman and it is almost a certainty he will receive the democratic nomination without opposition!" This he did and was later unopposed in the November election.

For a newcomer to the General Assembly of 1914, the young representative from Bourbon County received a proper welcome. Speaker of the House Claude Terrell placed him on several important committees and made him chairman of the Committee on Banks and Banking. But the committee that claimed his greatest interest was the one on Revenue and Taxation. Among the many bills he succeeded in getting passed was one calling for a uniform system of accounting in all state offices, the obvious purpose of which was to stop some of the graft going on in state government. In support of his bill Hutchcraft quoted the state treasurer as saying that the existing system of accounting made it possible for certain officials to "steal $100,000 of the state's money and there would be no way to catch them." Hutchcraft sided against a bill to give Kentucky a chance to vote on statewide prohibition in the 1915 election. He also voted against a bill to give women the vote, opposing the position of his sister, Mary Fithian Hutchcraft, who had become active in the suffrage movement, and of leaders such as Madeline McDowell Breckinridge of Lexington and her husband, the influential editor of the Lexington *Herald.* Undoubtedly opposing a sister who was held in high regard by her contemporaries left Hutchcraft with a heavy heart and some loss of self-confidence.

The year 1914 was an unhappy one for young Hutchcraft, perhaps partly because of his entanglement in several controversial political issues, but even more so because of the financial misfortunes of his father. Reuben Hutchcraft Sr. was a man of large and varied interests, mainly in land and the bluegrass seed business. He was a stockholder and director of a bank that went broke in those risky days of double liability for bank stockholders. Some of the Bourbon County aristocracy suffered indictments, but no personal scandal touched Hutchcraft.

On October 30, 1914, the elder Hutchcraft listed all of his property in an assignment for the benefit of creditors, showing assets in the amount of $215,600 and liabilities in the amount of $145,300. In today's world it would probably have been possible for him to extricate himself, but with the potential bank liability hanging over him, the best he could do was to try to be fair to all his creditors by making the assignment.

The same year, young Hutchcraft became deeply involved in a local option wet-dry election in which he represented the drys. The drys won, but the hard-fought controversy left bitter feelings and was projected into prolonged litigation. The drys finally prevailed in the Court of Appeals, and fifteen saloons in Paris closed.

Hutchcraft did receive his party's nomination for the legislature again in 1915, and again he was unopposed. But it was a different story in the November election. This time he had first-rate Republican opposition and narrowly scraped by with a margin of only fifty-six votes over N.A. Moore. In the same election, A.O. Stanley won a narrow victory over Republican Edwin P. Morrow for governor.

In the meantime Hutchcraft's law practice prospered, and he was made a director of the First National Bank and of the Bourbon Building and Loan. In Democratic politics he also moved forward to some extent, being made secretary of the county Democratic convention and a delegate to the state convention.

Nevertheless, it seemed that a bright political future was beginning to fade. Was it the press of other interests that permitted Claude Thomas to take Hutchcraft's seat in the legislature without a contest? Hutchcraft had developed interests other than politics, one of which was teaching law part-time at the University of Kentucky. He was also, for a time, a teacher in the Sunday school of the Paris Christian Church. But those interests seemed not enough to dim his abiding love of politics.

His last legislative duties were in a special session in early 1917. In May of that year he applied for admission to the Army's Officers' Reserve Corps and began active duty at Fort Benjamin Harrison, Indiana, on May 17, 1917. One of his last appearances before induction was at an evening session of his Masonic Lodge in Paris, where he occupied the Master's chair. In a few brief remarks he said, "I am going to France to fight, but somehow I feel I shall never return. I feel this is the last time I shall ever meet with you, my brothers, and this is the last address I shall make to you."

The speech to his Masonic brothers probably marked an all-time low for a young man accustomed to the plaudits of his contemporaries for an uninterrupted string of successes. As valedictorian of his class at Transylvania, associate editor of the prestigious *Harvard Law Review*, an unopposed easy winner of a 1913 election to the Kentucky General Assembly, his miraculous rise had seemed unending.

But things spiraled downward. Hutchcraft had accumulated enemies in the bitter wet-dry fight of 1914. His father went bankrupt. He barely squeaked by his Republican opponent in his race for reelection in 1915, even though Bourbon County was traditionally Democratic. These events in combination seemed to create a loss of faith in himself and produce his decision not to run again in 1917. Maybe, if he survived the war, he could begin again. Undoubtedly to restore his faith, Hutchcraft was determined to return to glory in the Great War. He succeeded in doing so.

On the night of November 6, 1918, Captain Reuben Brent Hutchcraft Jr. of Paris, Kentucky, and the men of Company K, 166th Infantry, were resting. They were part of the battle-weary Rainbow Division. They had been fighting for weeks in rain and mud near Sedan, France, in the great Meuse-Argonne offensive. That offensive, with enormous American losses, had pushed back the German forces and completely justified the faith of the American commander-in-chief, General John J. "Blackjack" Pershing.

General Pershing successfully opposed the efforts of the French and British commanders, who argued that the green American troops must be integrated with seasoned French and British units to withstand the horrors of combat and to meet the war-hardened forces of the Kaiser. Recent bloody offensives by the Americans along a thirty-nine-mile front previously held by the French had

been highly successful as more than 700,000 Yanks attacked the
Germans head-on. The fighting in those early days of November
1918 was north of Verdun in the region of the Argonne Forest and
along the Meuse River.

Captain Hutchcraft had just won a battlefield promotion from
first lieutenant and was given the command of a company commander who had been killed in action. That cold and rainy November night Hutchcraft and his men breathed more easily than they
had in weeks as they slept in a bombed-out church in LaNeuville, a
village about ten miles south of Sedan.

The offensive was approaching a long-sought victory that would
come unexpectedly only five days later with the signing of the armistice. But there was more fighting ahead. At 1:00 A.M. on the
morning of November 7, Hutchcraft was awakened and handed orders directing him and his company to resume battle immediately
and to continue the advance toward Sedan.

The order gave Hutchcraft the choice of how and with what
troops to resume action. The American forces had been stopped by
heavy machine-gun fire from a wooded knoll north of the village of
Chevauges. It was evident that the German guns must be silenced
or further advance would be impossible. The immediate need was
for a patrol to reconnoiter the position of the enemy guns so that
artillery fire could be called in to destroy them. An official report of
the 166th Infantry, 42nd (Rainbow) Division stated: "Hutchcraft
could have detailed an officer to lead the patrol. He chose to lead it
himself." Armed only with his Colt 45, Hutchcraft led the patrol up
the road toward the enemy. As the first daylight appeared, he and
his men passed through a small village and halted.

At this point Hutchcraft sent a scout back to reestablish contact with the main battalion to the rear. The survivor's notes state
that at that moment, "The rattle of machine guns told us we were
trapped." Hutchcraft ordered his men to dig in immediately along
the road. He called out, telling them they were in a trap and ordering them to make a good account of themselves. The survivor noted:
"We all knew and were determined to fight to the end for and with

him." Hutchcraft assumed he must personally locate the guns and find an opening in the enemy lines. While his men lay flat in their foxholes, he crawled out into the valley ahead. Immediately he was spotted and covered by enemy gunfire. A moment later his last words were, "They've got me, boys, but don't give up."

A surviving member of the patrol reported that six men were killed trying to reach him. Some while later, a seventh man succeeded, only to find his beloved captain dead. But in the fight the position of the German guns was spotted and they were wiped out. The battalion's advance that day was the deepest penetration of all the allied forces on the entire front. The next day the Americans took Sedan; three days later the armistice was signed and the war ended.

When Hutchcraft's body was recovered, it was taken to the small bombed-out church in LaNeuville where he and his comrades had rested the previous night. On the morning of November 9 burial was held in the churchyard and, as one of his American comrades said, "Those hardened veterans to whom death was a common sight cried like children." His body was soon moved to a cemetery between the towns of Beaumont and Letanne near the Meuse River. His friend and law school classmate Colonel Henry Breckinridge later visited his grave and wrote about the serenity and beauty of the spot, saying that Hutchcraft's body was "suitably interred in the fields he died to win."

At the opening of the 1920 session of the Kentucky General Assembly, on January 14, 1920, a memorial service for Hutchcraft was held in the House chamber. Honoring him at the service were Governor Edwin P. Morrow, all the members of the Court of Appeals, and both houses of the legislature. The American flag was draped over the desk once occupied by Hutchcraft as a band in the gallery played the national anthem. General Order Number 37 of the War Department, 1919, awarding the Distinguished Service Cross was read as follows:

> He personally took command of the platoon of his Company, which was designated as advanced guard, and led his patrol to the most

advanced point reached by any of our troops during the engagement. He was killed while making reconnaissance within 30 yards of enemy machine guns.

Posthumously awarded. Medal presented to mother, Mrs. R.B. Hutchcraft.

Speeches were made, resolutions passed, and many tears shed before Captain Hutchcraft's family left the chamber as the service ended.

On March 26, 1921, the body was returned to Paris, accompanied by a military escort from Fort Knox. Funeral services were conducted at the Paris Christian Church the following Sunday afternoon, still the largest service of its kind ever conducted in Paris. Representatives of American Legion posts from many counties in Kentucky were there. Also in attendance, in addition to family and friends, were large groups of Boy Scouts, the War Mothers, and many representatives of Masonic lodges. Judge Richard C. Stoll, president of the Fayette County Bar, led a delegation representing the Bar Association of Kentucky.

The Reverend W.E. Ellis, pastor of the Paris Christian Church, accompanied by the executive committee of the College of the Bible of Transylvania, conducted the services. Included in the Reverend Mr. Ellis's words were these: "Taking it all in all, I think it is the saddest death of any public man in the history of our great state."

The body of Captain Hutchcraft was thus put to rest at last in the soil of his own Bourbon County.

EIGHT

Prich

Edward F. Prichard Jr., known to us as "Prich," was easily the most famous of the friends I grew up with. To generations younger than mine, his name in Kentucky seems synonymous with education reform. But to those of us in his own generation who knew him, his life seems something of a Greek tragedy. It is difficult for me to write about him, and I would not, except that much of our lives and times were so close that for me to fail to do so would be, in legal terms, a "material nondisclosure."

When we were little boys, Prich and I used to visit each other, he on our farm in the country and I at his family's house in Paris. Our parents were friends. I think my parents thought more of Mrs. Prichard than of Prich's father. Mr. Prichard was a big, bullying, bullshitting kind of guy. Prich's mother was a very talented musician. Prich's younger brother, Henry Power Prichard, is a composer and pianist. As children we called him Power. I was amazed as a child to learn that Power had perfect pitch, a gift that amazes me still.

Prich and I were friends during most of our lives, with the usual disagreements that arise naturally from differences in personality. But for one period of more than twenty-five years there was sharp separation between us; that was the period from Prich's conviction for vote fraud in 1949 to the time in 1976 when he admitted his guilt to *Courier-Journal* writer John Ed Pearce.

It was not the crime itself that caused our break. Until 1976, Prich had stoutly claimed innocence and by doing so put himself in the position of making my father, whose testimony at the trial convicted him, appear to be a liar and a man who was out to destroy

him. So Prich and I had to be enemies. The situation was difficult
for us and for others, too. The people of Bourbon County and Central Kentucky who had been friends of both the Arderys and the
Prichards were forced to choose. There were those who knew Prich
was guilty, who saw nothing wrong with his denial of guilt, and who
thought the Arderys, particularly my father, then a judge, should
have no compunction about lying to protect him. Others sympathetic to Prich honestly thought him innocent and believed my father was trying to destroy a young man of great promise. Neither
group seemed to understand that Judge Ardery never volunteered
any testimony in the trial but only responded to subpoena, and even
then he did his best to claim privilege so as not to testify.

Then there were others of our acquaintance who felt Prich did
wrong, who understood that my father was forced to testify, and
who remained friends of the Arderys. Somehow, some of them continued to be friends with both the Arderys and the Prichards.

Many awkward situations arose. I remember one time when I
was in Bert Combs's office when he was governor. When Bert and I
finished our chat, the secretary came into the room and said, "Mr.
Prichard is in the outer office. Mr. Ardery, I thought you might like
to go out through the back door." I said, "Of course not. I have
nothing to be ashamed of." I walked by Prich as I went out and
looked at him. He didn't speak and neither did I.

Again, I was in the Washington airport late one afternoon. I
saw Prich waiting for the same flight returning to Kentucky. I happened to board the flight first. When Prich came down the aisle, he
looked as though he might speak, but neither of us did. Then, when
others were seated, he walked to the front of the airplane again and
returned. This time we both spoke. This sounds silly, I know, but to
some extent it characterized our relationship for a period of years.

As youngsters, Prich and I saw each other on visits, but perhaps our main relationship was through school. We both attended
the Paris public schools—grammar school, junior high, and high
school. We graduated in the same class, that of 1931. There was
never any doubt that Prich was number one in the class in all years,
and I think I was number two most of those years. The only courses

I beat him in were physics and chemistry. We were both on the debating team. Our debate coach was Zerelda Noland, an excellent teacher of English and a very good coach. Both Prich and I held her in the highest esteem. Both of us were pallbearers at her funeral many years after high school and after the tragedy of the vote fraud had occurred.

I'm sure Prich had as much advantage over me as a debater as he did in English classes. I was a slow starter as a debater, being burdened by more than the normal amount of stage fright, something that never seemed to bother Prich. Later I became captain of the University of Kentucky debate team, and Prich was captain of the Princeton team. The two teams met on one occasion in Paris High School auditorium before a large crowd, and I was pleased with the compliment Miss Noland paid me after the meet was over.

During our junior year in high school, Prich won a trip to Italy in a contest sponsored by the Mussolini government. As I recall, Il Duce was trying to improve his reputation among Americans. The contest, which was basically a general intelligence contest among American high school students, was set up and run by some American news organization, perhaps the Associated Press. Ten winners were to have an all-expense-paid trip to Italy awarded by the Italian government. I believe Prich was rated highest among the ten winners. I remember getting a postcard from him after he arrived in Rome: "Well, here I am in Italy where even the children speak Italian." The American students actually met with Mussolini, and Il Duce gave each of the young men an autographed picture of himself in a silver frame. As soon as he got back to his hotel, Prich tore up the picture and kept the frame. Later, he lost the frame.

Prich was indeed a brilliant young man, as the record shows. He was fat and rosy-cheeked and to some extent was made fun of by his contemporaries, perhaps from envy more than anything else. I know I thought him brilliant, but I would not have changed places with him because I cared about many things that didn't interest him at all.

After graduation, Prich entered Princeton while I went to the University of Kentucky. I would have liked to go to one of the Ivy

League universities, but those were Depression days and my parents were already supporting my two older brothers at UK. For the next four years, Prich and I saw little of each other except during summers.

When those years were over, both of us decided to go to law school. I'd made a good record at UK, being elected to Phi Beta Kappa and graduating with "high distinction." Prich's record was better at Princeton. He didn't make Phi Beta Kappa, and I never found out why, but he did graduate *summa cum laude*. We both wanted to go to the best law school in the country, and there was no doubt in the minds of either of us that that school was Harvard.

We both started the study of law in Cambridge in the fall of 1935. It was much more of a shock for me than for Prich because I had never really been out of the South before. In his four years in Princeton he had come in contact with many young men from the North and the East. And, too, several of the young men who had graduated with Prich turned up in our class at Harvard Law. Another new experience for me was competing with those who had graduated from prep schools like Groton, Exeter, and Milton. They were much better prepared than I; the main difference was that they had learned how to write exam papers and I never really had.

The first year at Harvard I let the school pick a roommate for me in one of the dorms. That was a real mistake. I never got along with my roommate. The next year Prich suggested we try rooming together in a dormitory at 99 Brattle Street made available to law students by the Episcopal Theological Seminary. Living in that dorm were several of Prich's old pals from Princeton. I found life at 99 Brattle Street much happier.

My grades that first year were about average. Prich's were much better, and he was asked to join the *Harvard Law Review*. I became reconciled to the fact that I wasn't going to establish an outstanding record as a legal scholar, and I took it easy and took up skiing, ice hockey, touch football, and softball, the latter two sports being played in the backyard of the Longfellow house next door to us.

The last two years at law school were a real joy. I gained a re-

Ed Prichard, in a sketch
by Phil Ardery, 1935.

spect for the law I'd never had before, even though it had always
been a part of my home environment. Frequently in the evenings
we would have Law Club meetings at which some distinguished
guest might be present. I remember one at which Samuel Williston,
a world-renowned expert in contracts, held forth. At another, Felix
Frankfurter, then professor of law at Harvard and later a Supreme
Court Justice, came and brought with him Harold Laski, who was
then the head of the British Labor Party. Those were, indeed, exciting times.

But during those days, Prich's cynicism seemed to grow. He
used to call me "A." After he had met someone who didn't impress
him, he would often say, "A, I'll bet that sombitch is too damn dumb
to be anything but honest." At other times, I recall his saying, "A, if
you had to be one or the other, which would you rather be, a dumb
fucker or a simple shit?" Such comments would come out with a
smile and usually produced laughter from his admirers. Prich's ap-
proval was much desired at the Lincoln's Inn where we spent most
evenings. A lot of guys felt it a privilege to eat at the same table
with Prich. Most of the faculty recognized him as someone of great
ability and unusual charm. He certainly could charm when he
wanted to.

We did have our arguments. One time I caught him opening a

letter of mine; Prich had a gnawing desire to know everything going on, including information to be found in my mail. But for the
most part, our relationship in law school was a happy one.

In the summers of 1936 and 1937, I landed a job as a law clerk
in a small Wall Street firm. Colonel Henry Breckinridge, a distant
relative of my father, helped me get it. We had a few select clients,
such as the Daniel Guggenheim estate, the Florida East Coast Railway, and the *New York World-Telegram*. I spent most of my time in
the library writing legal memoranda, but on weekends I had fun
visiting the Guggenheim estate on Long Island.

During those summer months of 1936 and 1937, I lived in a
one-room "apartment" at an old brownstone-front building at 14
East Sixtieth Street. That little hotel is long gone, and that address
is now the location of the Copacabana. One of the main advantages
of the location was that it was just a step or two away from the south-
east corner of Central Park. The Goldman Band held concerts in
the park in summer. There was also a small cafeteria overlooking
the pool where seals cavorted, and the smells of the menagerie
mixed, not unpleasantly, I thought, with the food. In those days,
the park was pure joy, not having the terror that today has destroyed
a large part of its charm.

During those two summers, I lost track of Prich. I'd come home
to Paris just a few days before departing for Cambridge to continue
law school. Prich was a complete politician, and I believe his summers were spent in furthering his already impressive grasp of the
science of politics. I know that, even after school started in 1936,
he spent many weeks in New Jersey, where he had become a valuable asset to the Democratic party's machinery in Trenton. He was
a thousand-percent Roosevelt man. I was a Roosevelt man, too, but
not as hardworking and effective as he.

At the time of our graduation from law school in 1938, I didn't
wait to get my diploma but went directly home to Kentucky and
had it mailed to me. Prich had been asked by Felix Frankfurter to
stay on another year and do some sort of graduate work. I planned
to start practice in Kentucky as soon as I passed the bar exam, and I
started studying for it as soon as I got home. Prich, as I recall, had

decided to delay taking the bar in order to give full attention to the job Frankfurter had laid out for him.

At the end of the summer of 1938 I passed the bar with little difficulty and started practice in Frankfort. Frankfort was a small town, but being the state capital it had more than the usual small town's amount of law work to be done, and I thought it was the town in Kentucky with the most opportunity for a lawyer at that time. I was offered a chance to go with the only group worthy to call itself a law firm, Smith and Leary, but with characteristic ego I decided to hang out my shingle and practice on my own. That idea didn't seem quite as ridiculous at that time as it would now. Starting with a group of mainly indigent clients, I managed to find my way around the courtroom. I tried a lot of jury cases, civil and criminal, and after a while began to think of myself as being reasonably well qualified in all phases of the profession. At least I was competent to handle the matters the country folk brought to me.

From 1938 to 1940, while I was learning the ropes of being a country lawyer, Prich was in Cambridge with Frankfurter. During his first year as a graduate student, Frankfurter was appointed to the Supreme Court and took Prich with him to Washington as his first law clerk. Shortly after that, Prich and several other bright young men rented a big house in Washington called "Hockley" that soon became the center of activity for many bright New Dealers. I think a number of people, including Philip Graham, Arthur Schlesinger Jr., and Adrian Fisher—the brightest and the best—either lived there or visited often. During those years, Prich and I corresponded at intervals but really had little continuing contact with each other.

As a result of my ROTC training, I had been commissioned a reserve officer in the infantry when I graduated from UK. In the summer of 1940 a lot of us were called up for three weeks of active duty for special maneuvers in Wisconsin. I'd been promoted to first lieutenant and hadn't given the military much attention until that call-up. The duty was miserable. I decided a war was coming, and I didn't want to get caught in the infantry. From here on for the next five years my story is best told in my book *Bomber Pilot*, an autobiography of my years in the military during World War II.

During those years I had no contact with Prich except for an occasional letter. I did get news about him from my family at home from time to time. Prich was called up by the draft, and his comment about being drafted, as quoted in the press was, "They've scraped the bottom of the barrel and now they're taking the barrel." He was soon classified 4-F, having failed his physical exam.

This caused only a brief interruption in Prich's Washington career, a career that became more dazzling all the time. After finishing his service as a law clerk for Frankfurter, he went on to work with Tom Clark, the attorney general. Another close friend of his was Paul Porter, who worked as a deputy administrator for the Office of Price Administration during the war and was also the top assistant to Kentuckian Fred Vinson, who headed the Office of Economic Stabilization, later was secretary of treasury, and later still became Chief Justice of the Supreme Court. Prich worked with Vinson during the days before his elevation to the Court. Prich's star continued to rise, and he became a legend around Washington as a raconteur, wit, and trusted counselor to the high and mighty.

Meanwhile, I completed a combat tour in Europe and the Middle East as a pilot, commander, and staff officer in the heavy-bomber operations of what was then the Army Air Corps, then returned to the states and became a wing operations officer at the Air Corps Tactical Center in Orlando, Florida. We took all the new aircraft, flew them, and developed the tactical doctrine to specify how such equipment would be used most effectively in combat. My service at Orlando was heavenly relief from the tensions of combat operations.

I had been at Orlando about a year when V-E Day arrived. It was certain that the vast military machine was about to be disbanded when one day I got a call from Washington. It was Prich. He said, "I'm going to leave this place very soon to return to law practice in Kentucky. I want you to come up here, and we'll see if we can work something out to practice together." This seemed an exciting prospect to me. I had a stripped-down B-25 at my disposal as wing operations officer. It was fast and completely trustworthy as an all-weather aircraft, and I loved flying it. So within a couple of days

I flew to Bolling Field, which was then the principal military base in the Washington area. At the base, I called for a staff car to take me to the White House, where Prich had his office in those days. Actually, it was Fred Vinson's office, but a visit there would make one believe it was more Prich's than Vinson's.

My car pulled up to the gate, and the White House guard stopped us. I said I had an appointment with Mr. Prichard. Immediately the gate was opened and my staff car rolled in. I was impressed, to say the least. I was ushered to the proper place, and there was Prich, with a big black cigar sticking out of the corner of his mouth, sitting behind Vinson's desk. His feet were on the top of the desk and he had the look of a man who was ruling the world.

We chatted amiably for a while and agreed that both of us would begin making arrangements to be relieved of present duties, go home, and get started in law practice under the name of Prichard and Ardery. He would have an office in Lexington and I'd have one in Frankfort. I would be in charge of finding secretaries and perhaps some other young lawyers to start with us. I had had some contact with Dean Evans of the UK law school, and I told Prich that as soon as I could I'd get his advice about younger graduates we might interview as associates.

That was the beginning plan of our new law firm. Soon after that I was released from active duty and returned to Kentucky. I went directly to see Dean Evans, and he recommended A.E. Funk Jr. as an associate. The dean said young Al was one of the brightest students to be graduated in years. Funk's father was the attorney general of Kentucky at that time. I had conferences with Charles Hobson, another recent graduate of the UK law school and a member of a family distinguished for having a number of fine lawyers. Hobson became my associate in the Frankfort office of Prichard and Ardery. Funk was Prich's associate in Lexington.

That was 1946, and a race for the U.S. Senate was about to begin. I had received a lot of publicity as a "war hero" and had pretty good name recognition throughout the state. I decided to try to cash in on that name recognition, and I tossed my hat in the ring for the nomination for senator. It seemed a pretty wild thing to do at that time, but I did pick up a good deal of support in a crazy primary in which there were eleven candidates. The one candidate who had more support than I was John Y. Brown Sr., whose son would become governor some thirty-three years later.

John Y. Brown had more support from the courthouse crowds around Kentucky than I did, but we ran a pretty close race. I don't recall the actual count, but I do remember that I carried the First, Third, and Sixth congressional districts. Brown carried the others and won the nomination but was beaten by Republican John Sherman Cooper in the November election. Prich supported me all the way through, although his close personal friend Earle Clements, a master politician who was elected governor the next year, started out for me and switched to Brown. I've always believed that, but for the Clements switch, I would have won the nomination for the Senate and beaten Cooper. When Cooper left the Senate many years later he wrote me a letter saying the same thing.

Losing the race led me to address myself more fully to the practice of law. But I couldn't do that entirely because Harry Lee Waterfield, who was mainly responsible for my carrying the First District in my race, was running that year, 1947, in the primary for governor against Earle Clements. Prich and I thought we could agree to disagree, but soon it became apparent that any such effort must fail if each of us was to give wholehearted and honest support to the candidate of his choice. So we split up. I kept the Frankfort office, and Prich kept the one in Lexington. I kept Hobson as my associate, and Prich kept Al Funk. Clements won the nomination and the election and became governor of Kentucky in December 1947. His election set Prich up as a top politician in Kentucky and one of the closest advisers to the governor. I had good prospects as a lawyer and really had no reason to complain. Hobson and I were beginning to build a good practice.

At the time of that election, I'd had little recent contact with Prich. He'd kept his voting residence in Bourbon County, and I had changed mine to Franklin. The election of November 2, 1948, was a fateful one in Bourbon County. On election day, Republican election officers, having been warned of possible irregularities, took the precaution of shaking the ballot boxes before the voting began. You'd think they would always do that, but apparently they had never done so before. In eleven precincts, the sound of ballots sloshing around in the boxes indicated that, indeed, something fishy was going on. The Republican election officers refused to allow balloting to begin in those precincts until further investigation had been made. It turned out that some 254 marked ballots were in the boxes of those eleven precincts, all marked for the straight Democratic ticket, except for one marked for John Sherman Cooper, who was running for a full term as senator after his election the year before to an unexpired term.

Before the day was out, the turmoil rocked Bourbon County and made the national press. The ballot boxes and voting paraphernalia from the eleven precincts were impounded. The vote in the other precincts in the county revealed a strong Democratic majority; in fact, the winning margin far exceeded the number of illegally cast ballots.

It was said by many that election irregularities were to be expected in Bourbon and many other counties in Kentucky. But the number of precincts affected as well as the number of illegal ballots cast did make this case unusual. It was known by nearly all in the county who paid any attention to elections that "Big Prich," Prich's father, "could handle" several precincts, including those known as Firehouse Nos. 1 and 2 and Clintonville Nos. 1 and 2. But having eleven of the county precincts affected was more than most people were accustomed to hearing about. Prich himself was an election officer at one of the precincts involved. Most people thought that, though the young man was "interested in politics," the actual chicanery, if there was any, was attributable to "Big Prich."

The general consensus, though, was that the Prichards were somehow responsible. At least, the Republican party representatives were so convinced. We Arderys heard it like everybody else, but we perhaps heard somewhat more because Harry Horton, Bourbon County Republican chairman, was a cousin of ours. Harry told us that the night before the election he received an anonymous phone call, long distance, which he believed came from Lexington.

The caller said, "You Republicans are too dumb to know what's going on in Bourbon County, and if you want to know what I mean, shake the boxes before you begin voting tomorrow." This story was circulated throughout the county. I never got any direct word from Prich about the election, but talk about the Bourbon County vote fraud continued to be a big story.

The matter just would not blow over. Cassius Clay, a distinguished Bourbon County lawyer who had served as general solicitor of the Rural Finance Administration in Washington and attorney for the B&O Railroad, organized a citizens' committee that demanded action. Since the election in question was a federal election, he called on the FBI to investigate. When the next regular grand jury meeting was to be held in the local circuit court, the question in many minds was, Will the local grand jury look into the matter? It was up to the judge to charge the grand jury. My father was the judge.

The grand jury was to convene Monday, November 8, the week following the vote fraud. On Sunday evening, after I had gone to bed quite early, I got a call from Lexington. It was Prich, wanting to know if he could come over that night and talk with me. I hadn't heard his voice in many months, but somehow the call didn't surprise me. In about forty-five minutes he showed up at my door in Frankfort. "I'm in a heap of trouble," he said, "and I need some advice." I let him in, and he continued, "My fingerprints are all over those ballots in Bourbon County, and I wonder if your father would be willing to talk to me about it."

My response was, "Prich, I don't know. It's pretty late, but I'll call him and ask." I called my father in Paris. He too was in bed, but he said, "Come on over." I thought I knew what my father would tell Prich because it would be the same thing he'd tell me if I were in the same kind of trouble. He would say, "You got yourself into this, now it's up to you to face it and walk straight out of it the way you walked into it." As we were driving to Paris I told Prich that I imagined my father would suggest that he admit what he had done and call on the people of the county, including Cassius Clay's citizens' committee, to forgive him for making a serious mistake and promise never to make that mistake again. I didn't get much response.

When we arrived at the house in Bourbon County, we went in through the back porch into the dining room, the usual course of entry. My mother was in a dressing gown and my father in casual attire, shirt and khaki pants. He and Prich went into the living room, leaving Mum and me in the dining room. I didn't hear what was said, but after about forty-five minutes Prich and my father reentered the dining room, and with very few words Prich and I got in the car and returned to Frankfort. On the drive back, Prich confirmed my guess. My father had told him that he had written a charge to be read the following morning directing the grand jury to look into the vote fraud. Prich also said my father made it clear to him that he should admit what he and the others had done and face the consequences.

In the course of driving from Frankfort to Paris and back, Prich had told me a few of the details about how he and his law associate had gotten the county attorney, William Baldwin, a longtime political ally and close friend, to open the vault where the ballots were kept. They had taken ballots from the Bourbon County courthouse to the Lexington law office, where they'd marked them, then returned them to Paris, where the marked ballots were placed in the ballot boxes. The whole operation seemed to me pretty big just to be a "childish prank," as some of Prich's friends called it.

On the drive back to Frankfort, Prich gave me the clear impression that he wasn't about to take my father's advice. He said my father had suggested that he make an appearance at a mass meeting to be held at the Bourbon County courthouse the following week to organize public demand for action. My father believed Prich had sufficient charm, when he wanted to use it, to go before the crowd, declare his guilt, and gain sympathy. But it was no go. Prich had powerful friends in Washington, including Tom Clark, the attorney general, Fred Vinson, soon to become chief justice of the Supreme Court, and even President Truman. He'd occupied a position of great power and refused to suffer the indignity of a public confession of guilt.

The next day the Bourbon County grand jury was given the charge and began its investigation by impounding the ballot boxes, the ballots, and the voting paraphernalia in question. Soon, however, federal authorities stepped in and took possession of those items. For a long time nothing was done. Cassius Clay continued to raise hell about the lack of action. He went to Washington to talk with Kentucky's representatives in Congress and sought unsuccessfully to meet with Attorney General Clark. Tension grew, and Clay made a statement that the federal district attorney was "guilty of incompetence or worse." That comment brought a libel action. It was dismissed after numerous other events in the drama had taken place, but for a time it made headlines.

While all this turmoil was going on, President Truman took time off from the White House to visit his winter hideaway in Key West. A number of his advisers, including Vinson and Clark, were reported to be with him. It was also reported that Prich visited Key West at that time. In any event, shortly after that, the federal grand jury was called into an extended session specifically to look into the vote fraud matter, and it quickly handed down indictments against Prich and Al Funk, Prich's law associate. William Baldwin, who was said to have played a part in the affair, was not indicted. A member of the grand jury was later heard to say that Baldwin was quite popular as a county attorney and for that reason was not indicted.

It is my belief that at the president's meeting with his advisers in Key West, he must have said to Tom Clark, "If you've got your foot on that vote-fraud case in Kentucky, I want you to take it off. I've stood all of that kind of trouble I need from the Pendergasts in Kansas City, and I don't want to go through the same kind of thing from Kentucky." Whether any such thing was ever said or not, shortly after the Key West meeting, the special federal grand jury investigation began.

During part of the time between the instruction of the Bourbon County grand jury and the indictment by the federal grand jury, the FBI was quite active. FBI men walking up and down the streets of Paris kept the town buzzing. My father and I talked about the matter. We were both determined to seek privilege not to testify because of the lawyer-client relationship. Prich had come to us for legal advice at a time when there was literally no other reason for him to communicate with us at all. But we knew without saying it that if we were required to testify, we would testify truthfully.

The fact of the matter is that the FBI got almost the whole story of what had happened on the first day of its investigation. Nearly everybody in Paris knew who had committed the vote fraud, and many told the federal agents in almost exact detail about Prich and his father "playing a tune" with certain precincts. I recently reviewed almost a thousand pages of FBI records of its investigation; it took me almost two years to get these papers produced under the Freedom of Information Act. They were of considerable value in showing how the FBI went about its work and what it was able to uncover. The trouble with what the FBI found was that very little of it was evidence that would be acceptable in court prosecution. The FBI information revealed that a number of those questioned said that Prich or his father or both had let it be known that they had powerful allies at the very top who could protect them. FBI director J. Edgar Hoover, in a number of the documents, seemed to take pleasure in calling these statements to the attention of Attorney General Clark, who must have experienced great uneasiness.

Cassius Clay and the Bourbon County Ministerial Association continued feeding the fire to the point that the local circuit court claimed its right to the return of the materials taken from it if the federal court had no plan to take action. But the newly extended federal grand jury did hand down sealed indictments the second week of May 1949. Among those who had been called to testify were my father, Cassius Clay, and Kentucky State Police Commissioner Guthrie Crowe. Crowe was called because, as it was later revealed, Prich had gone to him to ask that the state police lab conduct some tests to find out whether a person's fingerprints would show up on the kind of paper on which ballots were printed.

When news of the indictments was made public, Prich and Al Funk both proclaimed their innocence, and the matter proceeded promptly to trial. My father's claim of privilege was denied; he was required to testify. The court held that a judge may not maintain a lawyer-client relationship such as would justify refusal to testify. I was called to testify too, but my claim of privilege was allowed. The government produced considerable evidence about the forged handwriting, which seemed to show clearly that the writing on the back of the ballots was not that of the persons who were supposed to have signed their names.

On July 15, 1949, the trial jury returned a verdict of guilty against Prich and not guilty for Funk. Prich was sentenced to two years in the federal penitentiary and served five months of that sentence before being released by Christmas. Clemency was granted by President Truman.

Courier-Journal writer Hugh Morris, who covered the trial, told me he left the courtroom immediately after the verdict was announced and walked down the street stopping the first eight or ten people he met. He told them of the jury's verdict and asked for comment. Hugh said every one of the persons interviewed expressed satisfaction that Prich was convicted and Funk acquitted. This, I think, is a sad but reasonably accurate representation of the feelings of the people of Central Kentucky at the time. Prich had hurt a lot of local people by letting them know he felt intellectually superior. The truth is that he *was* intellectually superior to most.

Ever since the great vote fraud of 1948, people in Bourbon County have been puzzled about why it happened. It seemed such a crazy thing for a young man so full of promise to do. Many have said it was just a "childish prank"; others have asserted that vote fraud had become so routine in Kentucky elections as to be a matter of course. But such statements don't explain why Prich did it. I recall a comment by Mark Ethridge, publisher of the *Courier-Journal,* who was very fond of Prich. Mark, a New Dealer and Roosevelt fan, saw in Prich one of the bright young people who had had a lot to do with giving the New Deal its basic thrust. Mark said he thought the things that were wrong with Prich were almost entirely attributable to his father. It's interesting to me that Prich's father not only failed to inculcate certain basic values in his son but, as Prich grew to maturity, actually involved him in his own shady schemes. Having had a wonderful father who believed in beating into me some principles of basic honesty, I have little right to pass judgment on anyone lacking such an advantage.

But Ethridge was probably not just talking about Prich's up-bringing. It was evident, too, that Prich's business affairs were inextricably tied up with his father's. The story circulating around Bourbon County that seemed most plausible was that Big Prich had about $20,000 at 10 to 1 on what the Democratic majority in Bourbon County would be. I do know that one of Big Prich's delights was gambling. Lexington at that time was the seat of operations of a well known bookie named Ed Curd, who would make odds on anything. He was the one who corrupted the University of Kentucky basketball teams during the Rupp era by getting players to shave points. He would show up in the players' dressing room at half time to let them know what the point spread was. Not long after the Bourbon vote fraud, Curd was defendant in an unsuccessful lawsuit in which the plaintiff claimed a considerable sum due on an election bet. According to this theory, the warning telephone call to the Republicans the night before the election came from Curd.

Prich and his father were almost continually in difficulty with the taxing authorities, state and federal. Prich paid no state income tax during the war despite claiming Kentucky as his residence. The matter was called to his attention as a state tax deficiency when the war was over. Big Prich, then in the Kentucky legislature, got a resolution passed giving the sense of that body that Prich had intended to do nothing wrong. I believe Prich finally paid the amount claimed due the state. After Prich's release from the penitentiary, Big Prich was involved in an action by the IRS to get access to certain bank records. The IRS took the position that the financial records of father and son were so inextricably connected that "in order to get the correct tax liability of E.F. Prichard, Sr.," it was necessary to have those of E.F. Prichard Jr.

Prich probably learned a lot from his experience. Though until the day he died he displayed great self-confidence, I never heard him repeat his earlier comment, "I'll bet that sombitch is too damn dumb to be anything but honest." From the time Prich returned from his stay in the penitentiary to the time of his death, there was a noticeable change in him—less arrogance, less cynicism, less of the old acidity. He still had his enemies, and he made no bones about that. For example, he hated Happy Chandler and would make some rough comments about him. And there were others. But he seemed to understand the necessity of reining in his old tendency to say clever, cutting things about people just for laughs.

No doubt there were times while Prich was getting established again in law practice that he had a hard time making ends meet. He had a lot of friends who stood ready to help him, but I think he was often reluctant to accept the help offered. He was, during my whole acquaintance, a phenomenally poor money manager. At law school he commented that Phil Ardery could get by better on a shoestring than anybody he knew. I did know how to get by on less than many of my compatriots, and I surely could get by on less than Prich.

Another episode that occurred after Prich served his time and had reentered law practice throws some light on the way he lived. I had an old friend who was involved in a divorce action before the Fayette (Lexington) Circuit Court. He said he had turned over to Prich, counsel for the wife, a check in the amount of $5,000 in partial settlement of their domestic affairs, but Prich had not remitted the check or any part of it to his client. My friend asked me to bring suit against Prich. I told him I would under no circumstances ever take a case against Prich, but I also told him how I thought he might easily solve the problem without paying any lawyer a fee. I suggested he write to the bar association and ask to have its ethics committee look into the matter. That was the last I ever heard of it, and I concluded that my friend had followed my advice.

Despite many of his problems, Prich began to regain standing in the community. That standing was enhanced when Governor Edward T. Breathitt appointed him to the Council on Higher Education in 1966. Several years later the council produced a report largely from Prich's work, and the Prichard Committee for Academic Excellence was formed and is still at work. As a principal political strategist for six of Kentucky's governors, his esteem in the minds of many Kentuckians was largely restored.

Ed Prichard, 1994. Courtesy of the *Courier-Journal.*

My last close association with Prich was when our class of 1938 at the Harvard Law School was about to have its forty-fifth anniversary reunion. Dunbar Holmes, one of our favorite classmates, was in charge of the reunion. He knew that Prich had suffered serious loss of eyesight because of a diabetic condition, but he was hopeful that he could attend the reunion. Dunbar wrote me asking if I thought I might get Prich to go. I called Prich and said I would be glad to go with him, look after him on the plane, and help with his housing accommodations. Prich said he'd like to go. His wife, Lucy, was somewhat more dubious, but we decided we could swing it. I made all the reservations, and we attended the reunion together. I was with him all the time except for a brief period while he was in dialysis at a Boston hospital.

Prich seemed to enjoy the reunion greatly. At a luncheon meeting, Harvard Law Dean Vorenberg made several complimentary references to him, and at the evening dinner meeting at the Boston Harvard Club, Prich was called on to speak briefly. At my suggestion, Dunbar, who was in charge of the dinner, gave Prich credit for having stirred Kentucky politicians into greater action to improve public education in Kentucky than had been the case in many years. And so, on the whole, I think Prich's trip back to Harvard was a happy one. We had several long conversations in our room. I enjoyed those conversations and from them was convinced that Prich's years after his conviction were the finest ones of his life. I continually reflect that the advice my father gave him before the vote-fraud investigation officially began was the same advice he would have given me had I found myself in similar circumstances. And I believe that if Prich had taken that advice, his story would have been a very different one.

NINE

Barton Stone and Cane Ridge

It must have been about seventy years ago that I first heard the name Barton Stone. It was in the very biblical surroundings of the parsonage occupied by my grandparents, the Reverend and Mrs. I.J. Spencer of Central Christian Church in Lexington. Stone, it seemed to me, was like St. Peter, to whom Jesus said, "Thou art Peter. On this rock will I found my church" (Matt. 11:18). And indeed, as I would later learn, what St. Peter was to the Roman Church, Barton Stone must have been not only to grandfather's church but to the worldwide denomination to which it belongs. In 1828 Stone purchased a lot on Hill Street in Lexington for a church building that was the predecessor of the church where my grandfather was later the minister.

"Brother Spencer," as my grandfather was called, was born in 1851, just fifty years after the "Great Revival" at Cane Ridge in Bourbon County. From an early age I heard about the revival meeting and the subsequent wranglings of pioneer theologians—mostly Presbyterians, but also including many dissident Baptists—that gave us our Christian Church, also called Disciples of Christ and, in my youth, pejoratively called "Campbellites." Grandfather Spencer and his devoted wife, Sally Louise Pendleton Spencer, saw to it that my brothers and I as little boys were given a strong foundation of Christian belief and an understanding of the particular kind of faith established by Barton Stone.

The parsonage where my grandparents lived was just behind the church on Walnut Street in Lexington. It smelled different from what I was accustomed to. The parsonage was darker and damper and lacked the warm smells of the kitchen or the animals about it that our farmhouse had. On the walls hung pictures of saints or of events from Bible stories.

I remember swinging my legs back and forth without ever touching the floor under the hard oak pews as I sat with my mother and grandmother toward the front of the church to hear Grandfather's Sunday sermon. The pews, of golden oak, were very much the same color as the furniture in the parsonage. The furniture in our house in Bourbon County was walnut and mahogany or some other dark-colored wood.

Grandmother Spencer taught Sunday school and was a real Bible scholar. Over and over she told me stories from the Old Testament. I remember the remarkable ability of Daniel to survive in the lions' den, and how Shadrach, Meshach, and Abednego were unharmed by the fiery furnace into which they were thrown by King Nebuchadnezzar. At mealtimes each of us was expected to recite a bit of Scripture, and I recall getting by more than once by reciting the shortest verse in the New Testament: "Jesus wept" (John 11:35).

I remember as well a vague impression I received of some slight feeling of competition, not quite conflict, between my grandfather Spencer's Christian Church on Walnut Street and that of "Brother Collis" on Broadway. The former was somehow more "liberal" and sided with Transylvania University and the College of the Bible (now Lexington Theological Seminary) whereas the latter was more fundamental or conservative, although of course I did not really know what the words "fundamental" or "conservative" meant. The Stone-Campbell effort really resulted over the years in three churches: the Christian Church (Disciples of Christ); the Christian Church, a more conservative denomination; and later on the Church of Christ, a still more fundamental branch.

The *History of Central Christian Church* (1962) by William Clayton Bower indicates that "membership when Dr. Spencer assumed the pastorate was 845; when he relinquished his ministry, it was 2,096. He had received into Central approximately 4,000 people." When the Spencer ministry ended, Central Christian had the largest membership of any church in Lexington; until recently it was still the largest Disciples of Christ church in Kentucky.

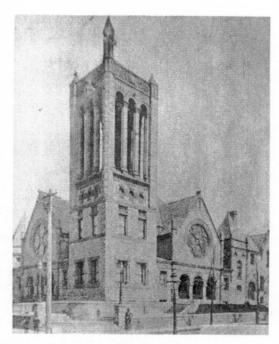

Central Christian Church, Lexington, built 1877.
Courtesy of Central Christian Church

For many years my mother was a devoted member and Sunday school teacher at the Paris Christian Church as well as a dedicated worker for restoration of the Cane Ridge church in Bourbon County. The log meeting house at Cane Ridge was built in 1791, when the area was still a part of Virginia, one year before Kentucky became a state. The story of Cane Ridge and Barton Stone, the "rock" on which our church was founded, evolved in my mind over many years. Later, after some research, I resolved to write about it.

Robert W. Finley, Princeton graduate from Bucks County, Pennsylvania, was a Presbyterian minister who moved to North Carolina in 1784. There he met Daniel Boone, who told him about the marvelous richness of the area that later became known as Cane Ridge. The abundant cane stood in places as high as ten feet and spread over an area fifteen miles long at considerable width. The growth remained green and succulent the entire year, providing forage for buffalo, deer, and elk, as it promised to do for cattle. Finley and others moved to that area in the 1780s and formed a tiny settlement about seven miles northeast of Paris, the newly established county seat of Bourbon County, then part of Virginia and soon to be part of Kentucky.

In 1791, the pioneers at Cane Ridge cut huge blue ash logs to construct the church, about fifty feet long and thirty feet wide, that stands restored on the spot today. Originally the logs were not chinked with clay so worshipers within could see any Indians who might attack. In mid-prayer a pioneer might reach for the long rifle between his knees if he saw a suspicious stirring in the shrubbery outside. The pulpit was in an alcove and raised several steps above the level of the congregation. A gallery looked down on the main congregation and could be reached by a ladder. The original floor was dirt, and the windows were without glass.

Young Barton Stone came to Cane Ridge as its first regular pastor in 1798; from the time of his arrival, he was immensely popular. Born in Maryland in 1772 and baptized into the Anglican faith, he had studied first for a career in law. Later he changed to the ministry and in 1796 received a license to preach at the Presbytery of Orange, North Carolina. When later ordained by the Presbytery of Transylvania, he accepted the Presbyterian Westminster Confession of Faith, adding, "in-so-far as I find it consistent with the will of God." In experience in his profession, he was older than his twenty-six years would make him appear.

Before leaving North Carolina, Stone had fallen under the influence of a religious zealot, James McGready, a teacher at the Guilford Academy. Of McGready's preaching at Guilford, Stone wrote, "Such earnestness, such zeal, such powerful persuasion, enforced by the joys of heaven and the miseries of hell, I have never witnessed before." McGready had come to Kentucky in 1796 and with his followers organized a number of revivals. Learning of the excitement produced by several of McGready's revival meetings, Stone traveled from Bourbon County to attend one in the spring of 1801 in Western Kentucky's Logan County. The trip from Cane Ridge to Russellville, the Logan County seat, a distance of nearly

Old Cane Ridge Meeting House, built 1791.

two hundred miles, took about seven days depending on stops along the way. According to historians, Logan County had earned a reputation as a "rogues' harbor" full of thieves and ruffians of all sorts; it was to saving the super sinners there that James McGready and his associates addressed themselves. Barton Stone came and saw and was much impressed. Having seen conversions that caused the converted to fall as though dead, then rise and shout hosannas to proclaim their love of Jesus, Stone wrote that he was sure it was "the work of God."

He returned to Bourbon County filled with enthusiasm as he made his report of the event to his Cane Ridge congregation and began planning for an important event to be held the "Friday before the third Lord's day in August" 1801. Only a little more than a month before the Great Revival, on July 2, Stone married Elizabeth Campbell. Thus, events of that summer and early fall were full to overflowing for the young minister.

On that Friday, August 8, 1801, the area around Cane Ridge Church was clear and leveled for perhaps two or three hundred yards. It was shaded and well adapted for the purpose of the re-

Barton Stone.

vival. The revival in Logan County had convinced Stone that he should expect an enormous crowd. One large tent was erected as shelter from heat and rain, and the ground around it was laid off in streets for the pitching of tents and the parking of wagons. On Friday the crowd began to arrive. At its peak, it was estimated to be from twenty to thirty thousand, the figure having been given by "a Revolutionary officer accustomed to estimate encampments." Some historians consider this estimate too high.

However accurate or inaccurate the estimates of the crowd may have been, there is little doubt that this was the greatest of the numerous revival meetings of that period on the frontier. Apparently word of mouth, stimulated by previous revival meetings, alerted religious enthusiasts. Witnesses told of the roads jammed with wagons, carriages, horsemen, and persons on foot moving into the camp. It was said that eighteen Presbyterian ministers were counted, along with many Baptist and Methodist preachers. The revival lasted the better part of a week, until all provisions gave out. The size of the meeting might be compared interestingly to the entire population of Bourbon County according to the latest census; that number in 1790 was 7,800.

The great Bourbon County revival of 1801 came at the beginning of a schism in the Presbyterian Church. Not surprisingly, the Presbyterians give a slightly different version of the events from those reported by Stone and his followers. One Presbyterian historian has said: "No wonder that multitudes drawn together by various motives should fall under the powerful spell of such an occasion." Another version states that "at times the scene was surprisingly terrible and the boldest heart was unmanned."

A more recent historian has commented on aspects of the Great Revival somewhat beyond the reports of Stone and the other supporting clergy. As might be expected, the crowd drew many unrepenting sinners. There were whiskey dealers who "carried on a lucrative business, and prostitutes were present for whatever trade was worth." Also, as typical for Kentucky, "politicians arrived early in the morning, the large crowds of receptive listeners offering opportunities too rare to miss."

Such reports bring to recollection a comment made by one of my elderly cousins when I was still a small boy. He said that his idea of heaven was to sit on his front porch in a straw-bottomed rocker on a summer Sunday afternoon, with "a mint julep in my hand, listening to a good preacher preach." Professor Thomas D. Clark, a great historian and a keen student of Kentucky character, appropriately observes that "among many Kentuckians, whiskey drinking, horse racing, and punctual attendance at church meetings can easily be reconciled." One of the repentant sinners at the Cane Ridge revival meetings, in telling of the shock of being suddenly saved, said that his feelings became so "intense and insupportable" that he found it necessary to "alley [sic] them by a dram of brandy."

There is no doubt that the Cane Ridge meeting of August 1801 was the greatest of the series of camp meeting revivals during the period from 1787 to 1805. "The noise was like the roar of Niagra [sic]. . . Sometimes hundreds were swept down at once. . . . Seven ministers, some in wagons, others standing on stumps, might have been counted, all addressing the multitude at the same time." Historian John B. Boles says the Great Revival "altered the course of Kentucky and southern history . . . never again was Protestant dominance threatened in the South." Naturally, the event leaves one with numerous questions, chiefly, what was it all about? There were signs of divergence from the traditional path within the Presbyterian Church and serious split-offs from the Baptist Church. Barton Stone had given some hint of the potential for dissent in his qualified acceptance of the Westminster Confession when he added, "in-so-far as I find it consistent with the will of God."

The Springfield Presbytery, organized by Stone and four others in 1803, was a dissident group whose progressive, or at least divergent, views led in 1804 to its formal dissolution. Its "Last Will and Testament" declares, "We *will*, that this body die, be dissolved and sink into union with the Body of Christ at large; for there is but one Body, and one Spirit, even as we are called in one hope of our calling." The document further declares that the power of making laws for the government of the church and of executing them by delegated authority shall "forever cease" and that all must "take the Bible as the only sure guide to Heaven." It encouraged the destruction of "partyism" and purportedly "freed" all who had been declared heretic for departing from the Presbyterian Confession of Faith. Barton Stone and five others previously prominent in the Presbyterian Church signed "The Last Will and Testament of the Springfield Presbytery" on June 28, 1804, almost three years after the great Cane Ridge revival. These dissenters were called "New Lights."

Stone had visions of a movement that would unify all Christian believers, but he was soon disappointed. The Shakers sent missionaries to Kentucky from New York in 1805, and several of Stone's more radical allies joined them. The Shakers believed the millennium had already begun and that Jesus Christ had returned to earth in the form of a woman, their leader, Mother Ann Lee. The Shaker communities of Pleasant Hill in Mercer County and South Union in Logan County, established in 1806, drew off some of the most extreme followers of Stone and may have influenced him, as a defensive measure, to join a movement similar to his own headed by Alexander Campbell. The transition spread over a period of years, and some historians believe the Shaker movement may have helped Stone by drawing off some of the more radical elements troubling him.

Alexander Campbell, educated at the University of Glasgow, Scotland, was the son of a Presbyterian minister who had left the Presbyterian Church. The Campbells, who preached in western Pennsylvania, based their faith solely on their interpretation of the New Testament. Campbell and his father called themselves Christian reformers. Because they believed total immersion was the only biblical form of baptism, they affiliated for a time with the Baptist Church, but always with reservations. Although Alexander was editor of the *Christian Baptist,* the Campbellite Reformers were too radical for the Baptists, so about 1830 they parted company. Meanwhile, a meeting in 1824 between the Barton Stone group and the Alexander Campbell group revealed their similarities. Stone was less flashy than Campbell and somewhat suspicious of the latter. The Stone group was the more revivalist of the two. But apparently Stone, having hoped for great ecumenicity and seeing folly in further splits, guided his followers into a loose alliance in 1832 at a meeting at Hill Street Church (later Central Christian) in Lexington. The two groups at the time had a total of about 22,000 members. The combination, calling itself after the Campbell group, Disciples of Christ, grew by 1860 to number some 192,000, of whom about 45,000 were Kentuckians. Thus the sprig of growth planted at Cane Ridge in 1801 had become a significant part of American Protestantism.

Stone and Campbell had ushered in a new, completely American sect. Their followers abjured "Calvinism," which meant they rejected all man-made creeds and depended entirely on the Bible, and chiefly on the New Testament, as the only expression of God. Alexander Campbell brought into the belief "total immersion" as the only proper means of baptism. (Stone himself was rebaptized by being totally immersed in Stoner Creek in Bourbon County.) The baptism of infants was definitely forbidden, as well as any Presbyterian notion about predestination. The new faith included weekly communion, open to all believers.

The ecumenism, the reliance on the Bible as the only Word, the doctrine of total immersion, and other aspects of the new religion also appealed to many Baptists, and there were numerous instances of entire Baptist congregations either leaving or being expelled from the Baptist Church for "heresy." Indeed, it has been said the Baptists were the "most vulnerable." The Tates Creek Baptist Association excluded many of its churches in Madison County. Similar disruptions occurred at Coopers' Run in Bourbon County and elsewhere around the state.

During the period shortly after the revival at Cane Ridge, other dissident groups appeared. The Cumberland Presbyterian group broke from the Kentucky Synod of the Presbyterian Church in 1810, and, as has been said, the Shakers were settling in with numerous more radical adherents of other churches. Here it is interesting to note that the local newspapers in publication at the time, including the famed *Kentucky Gazette* of Lexington, carried little or no news about the Great Revival of 1801 and the events that followed. The contemporary local press was almost entirely occupied with such matters as Napoleon in Egypt, or the Barbary pirates in the Mediterranean Sea, as well as national and local political news. The lack of press coverage at the time is quite amazing considering the lasting effects the events had on religion. The public gave little attention to the fact that during the year of the outbreak of the War of 1812, Stone sold his farm in Kentucky and moved his family to Tennessee, where they remained through 1814.

In 1815 Stone moved back to Kentucky, this time to live in Lexington, where the following year he founded what became the Hill Street Church. During these years the question of the Christian morality of slavery grew increasingly controversial. Stone freed his two slaves, Ned and Lucy. Negroes were members of Stone's early Cane Ridge church as well as the Brush Run, Pennsylvania, church

of Alexander Campbell before the Stone-Campbell union. Both
Stone and Campbell opposed slavery but did not refuse fellowship
to slave holders. This was consistent with Stone's general policy of
avoiding doctrinal rigidity. It also seems to correspond with the situation in other Protestant denominations at the time; though many
southern ministers had antislavery sentiments, most congregations
did not respond with wholehearted support.

When the movement to establish a black colony on the west
coast of Africa became popular (the Kentucky Colonization Society
was organized in 1828), both Stone and Campbell supported it. Although there were no doubt sharp differences of opinion within
the Stone-Campbell movement, the Disciples of Christ did not fall
victim to a "slavery schism" like those that overtook the largest Protestant denominations during the 1840s.

While the argument over slavery was waxing hotter and hotter,
a scourge of Asiatic cholera broke upon Kentucky like a mighty hur-
ricane. One of Stone's staunchest followers, clergyman John Rogers,
a native Kentuckian and one of the best writers of the time, de-
scribes returning to Kentucky after a mission visit to Ohio in 1833:
"I came through Lexington the day after the cholera broke out in
that city. All looked thoughtful & serious—a deep gloom hung over
the City, & the whole country. . . . It was no use to go into the re-
gions where cholera prevailed, as none would go to meeting. I continued, therefore, to preach at home, & in the neighborhood till
the cholera broke out in our village [Carlisle, in Nicholas County]
after the middle of June."

Rogers described how the disease spread and killed many "a
few hours after the attack." The fear of contagion was so great that
there was frantic haste to bury victims immediately after they died,
"so there remains little doubt that some, perhaps not a few, were
buried alive." When cholera came to Carlisle, many residents left,
and Rogers had to decide what arrangements to make for himself,
his wife, and his six children. "I felt as if it would be a cowardly act
in me to leave, & that, in the event of my surviving the cholera, I
could not return to my people, & preach to them. I resolved, therefore, that live, or die, for my own sake, the people's sake, & above

all—for Christ's sake, I would stay, & do what I could for my family
& the community."

Stone too had remained in Kentucky and was living at this time
in Georgetown, publishing the *Christian Messenger,* a strong antislavery paper. The next year, 1834, he moved to Jacksonville, Illinois, where he continued preaching.

The Cane Ridge meeting house was some thirty years old before any substantial changes were made to it. At that time there
was an appeal from William Rogers, an original officer of the church,
for the purpose of paying for the grounds of the church and adjoining burial ground and to make certain improvements so that the
building would be more comfortable during inclement weather.
Rogers's papers indicate that the church was to be "conveyed to the
Christian and Presbyterian Churches, but free for other societies
to worship in when not occupied by these churches." These changes
were consistent with Stone's ecumenism. One clergyman of the sect,
the Rev. Rhodes Thompson, in *Voices From Cane Ridge,* tells us
that the Rogers appeal resulted in the outside being "weather-
boarded, the walls inside were lathed and plastered," and the seats
were made more comfortable. The proceeds of the appeal also paid
for a lot of four acres including the building and adjacent grave-
yard.

Barton Warren Stone, who had suffered a stroke three years
earlier, died in Illinois on November 9, 1844, in his seventy-second
year. By that time, his biographers report, his handsome features
were changed, his dignified and manly bearing gone, his auburn
locks faded, his eyes dimmed, his cheeks furrowed and careworn.
Still, he was the greatly loved man who so many years before had
exhorted thousands to religious fury around the old log meeting
house, beside which he now lies buried. That was in accord with
the wish he had expressed when he left for Illinois.

In the more than two hundred years of Bourbon County history, Stone may have sparked the event having the greatest lasting
consequence. From the day the Christian Church began, there have
been divisions, and to that extent Stone's vision of complete church
unity has been dimmed. But recent statistics indicate that the total

numbers within the branches attached to the trunk of the Christian Church probably exceed three million throughout the world. Its affiliated institutions cover some twenty-four colleges, universities, seminaries, and seminary associates, including Kentucky's Transylvania University, the Lexington Theological Seminary, and others scattered from Texas Christian University to the Yale Divinity School.

In the introduction to Stone's *History of the Christian Church in the West,* Hoke Smith Dickinson writes, "Branded as a heretic because he could not wholly accept the creedal statement of his church and insisted on the primacy of the New Testament scriptures; branded as a rebel because of his revolt against narrow sectarianism, [Stone], nevertheless, had the faith and courage to wear with honor both brandings." Thus, it might be said that he was like the stone the builders rejected that became the cornerstone of the temple.

TEN

❧

Cap'n

His name was Willis Barton, but the three Ardery children called him Cap'n. We never knew how he got such a dignified name as Willis Barton because we never knew who his parents were, and if he ever knew, he never spoke about them. My earliest recollections of him must have been when he was about sixty years old, and to me that seemed very old. He did say he didn't remember when the men went away "to waw" (the Civil War), but he did remember when they "come home." That is how we guessed his age. He was totally without formal education and could neither read nor write except with some pride to write the name "Willis Barton." He never married and had no children to speak of.

Cap'n was handsome, with a face that looked like it might have been carved out of old walnut. He stood about five feet ten inches, almost the same height as my father, and he walked erect with the dignity of carriage of one who has worked hard all his life and has nothing to apologize for. The most persistent picture that remains in my mind is that of Cap'n in what he called "gum boots" with felt linings. He nearly always wore "overhauls" with a blue shirt, flannel in winter and cotton in summer.

What I remember most is his kindness. If the definition of a gentleman is a gentle man, he met that definition perfectly. I spent much more time in his company than my two older brothers did, but we all saw him as a loving member of the family despite the fact that he was, as we said in those days, "a colored man."

It is surely difficult for anyone growing up under different cir- cumstances than mine to understand our feelings about a black we truly loved. Cap'n had been born a slave of my great-grandfather,

Cap'n.

Lafayette Ardery, who died long before I was born. What I knew about him was mostly from stories I heard from Cap'n. He'd say, "Ole Lafayette had a high voice, lak a woman. But nobody couldn't take nothin' from him. Did, he'd be settin' in the fence corner at midnight." I could imagine the old man settin' in the fence corner at midnight. I never quite understood what the purpose of that was, but that was the way Cap'n told it to me, and that was the way I believed it.

Cap'n lived in a cabin across the road from our house. He had a yard that fenced in the numerous chickens, guineas, ducks, and geese he raised for his own purposes. His place was always neat and well tended. His cabin had no running water; an outhouse and a chicken house stood in the rear.

On early winter mornings Cap'n would be the first one moving around in the "big house." I would hear him making a fire in the living room fireplace and would get out of bed and rush to his side, freezing in my pajamas, as he first put paper, then kindling, then large lumps of coal in the grate. I'd say, "Hurry up, Cap'n, I'm freezing." Moments later the blaze would be leaping up the chimney and I'd back away. Cap'n would laugh and say, "Set up to it! Set up to it! You been hollerin' how cold you is. Now set up to it!" This scenario was played out between us dozens of times with joy and excitement.

Then he would proceed to make the fire in the large coal stove in the kitchen, assuring me that soon I would have eggs and bacon and milk and cornmeal batter cakes and all the other good things that went to make up breakfast. I knew perfectly well that without Cap'n, none of these nice things would happen.

As winter days usually went, after breakfast Cap'n and I would walk down across the road to the barn, where he would hitch up Pete and Jane, our mules, to the slide. The slide was a kind of sled used in the winter to haul fodder from the back of the farm to the front pasture, where the cows were. They had to have their breakfast, too, and from the amount of mooing and bellowing, they made it known that they got just as hungry as we did.

We had numerous dogs during my childhood, but the principal ones were two German shepherds, male and female, named Jerry and Flap. They were rabbit chasers whose only purpose was their own pleasure as farm dogs. Cap'n's personal dog was a real shepherd, something like a small collie, named Flu. She got her name from a wave of influenza that arrived at the same time she did. Flu worked hard rounding up cows and the other livestock to be brought into the barn. She was extremely well trained. She knew exactly what Cap'n expected of her and applied herself to her tasks with speed and a single-mindedness that was astounding.

While Pete and Jane were pulling the empty slide out to pick up the load of fodder, Flu would usually trot along between and a little bit behind them under the harness and beside the doubletree. Jerry and Flap would forage afar, sometimes scaring a rabbit out of its bed but always skimming the ground with their noses for anything they might find interesting. It seemed that polecats were always interesting, and that was why so often they smelled slightly skunky.

The field at the back of the farm was usually a cornfield, though sometimes the corn was rotated with tobacco. Often would be fodder shocks—stacks of cut corn—scattered around the field looking like so many wigwams. Beside one of the many fodder shocks Cap'n would stop the mules, and we'd pull down armloads of cornstalks and throw them on the bed of the slide. Sometimes when we tore into a fodder shock a rabbit would come dashing out, to the utter delight of Flap and Jerry. Those two dogs were excellent rabbit chasers, but the rabbits seemed to know a lot about being chased. It took real experience to catch a rabbit. Usually one of the dogs would overtake its quarry and be about to grab it when the rabbit would make a sharp turn to the right or left, leaving the dog far enough behind so that the rabbit could escape through a nearby fence.

Soon Cap'n would turn the slide, loaded high with stalks of corn, and head back to the front pasture and its herd of hungry cows. At about this point, my gun often claimed my interest. When I had grown up a bit, I was entrusted with a .22 caliber rifle, a Remington automatic, which really meant semiautomatic. There were only certain things I was allowed to shoot. Crows were fair game because they stole Cap'n's baby chicks. But crows were canny birds. They seemed to know when a rifle was anywhere near, and the only shots I got were pretty much out of range. I remember getting Cap'n to stop the slide one time to let me take aim at a crow high atop an old elm tree. The crow saw me and obviously thought it was safe. Cap'n let me know he thought I was wasting his time; but I took careful aim, allowing slight elevation and windage with the open sight, and killed the bird at a distance I stepped off at 133 yards. Unusual, to say the least.

Arriving at the front pasture, Cap'n would wrap the reins around a pole stuck in the front corner of the slide, and together we'd throw out the corn, armload after armload. The cattle would follow the slide, eating their breakfast with as much relish as I had mine.

Of those days with Cap'n, the ones I remember best are when I was a little boy, five to ten years old. Those winter days when there was snow on the ground and we hauled things around on the farm on the slide are matched with sunny recollections of summer days when Pete and Jane were hitched to a two-mule wagon for such things as hauling gravel from the gravel beds of Houston Creek.

We used the gravel on the grand circle of our driveway. The driveway was especially important to what I considered the imposing appearance of our house.

Houston Creek, fed by several cold-water springs, meandered generally northward about a quarter of a mile behind our house through the farm of our friends, the Brennans. It had lots of riffles and eddies and some deep holes, such as the one we swam in. The sandbanks in places were beautifully brown and smooth until the wagon pulled up to load gravel, making deep ruts that looked like cuts in caramel pie. Cap'n would take a big scoop shovel and load the wagon to what he considered the limit of the mules' capacity. Sometimes his shovel would bring up turtle eggs as white and round as ping-pong balls.

But the thing I remember most about hauling gravel was that only then did I see Pete and Jane put to the limit of their strength. Cap'n would shout at them, mostly Jane, by name. She was larger than Pete, but Cap'n knew she was lazy. He said she had a clever way of keeping the trace chains tight without really doing her share of the pulling. He said if he wasn't careful, Pete would do all the work. Maybe that was just male chauvinism on Cap'n's part, but I don't think so. He understood the workings of a mule's mind better than anyone I ever saw. He had a whip, and though he didn't use it often, the mules knew he had it.

During the days we spent together, I learned a lot of philosophy from the old man. On one occasion there had been an uproar in our household when our cook, Clara, was nearly killed by her indignant lover, Uley Monday. Uley and Clara weren't married, but most of the time they lived together in a cabin behind our house. On this particular occasion, Uley had been gone for about a week and returned to find what he thought was unmistakable evidence that Clara had been paying attention to another man. Uley took a pistol and shot Clara. The shooting wasn't fatal, but Uley evidently felt his point had been sufficiently made, and little came of the incident beyond talk among the other servants.

Cap'n's view of the event was, "He didn' have no right to shoot her. She didn' b'long to him!" The implication was that if they had been married, the action Uley took would have been perfectly proper. If the thing had ever come to trial in one of our local courts, my guess is that the jury would have found exactly according to Cap'n's view of the law and the facts.

His matter of factness came out in our conversations many times. I can recall several occasions in late winter, say late February or early March, when my impatience for the arrival of spring was particularly acute and I would ask him, "Cap'n, do you think we'll have any more snow?" His reply was always the same, "I dunno. I seed it snow the twentief of May." My father confirmed that he too remembered the famous snow on the twentieth of May from his boyhood. The snow fell heavily in the morning, he said, but then the sun came out and it was nearly all gone by the end of the day.

Another bit of the old man's philosophy, told me by my father, was from the early days when hemp was our farm's main crop. Cap'n would work extremely hard breaking hemp, then take his small pay to Paris on Saturday and buy drinks for his friends at Bud Macon's pool hall, the local gathering place for most of the colored folk. Cap'n had his own pint bottle that he'd take to be filled with Bourbon at the going rate of twenty-five cents. His comment, according to my father, was a bit of pure Cap'n philosophy: "What's the use of bein' a po' man all your life when you can be rich for a quarter?"

During the week, Cap'n's only point of social contact other than with house servants and farmhands was with young ladies, who would occasionally come to visit him from Paris. They would appear at the interurban streetcar stop near his house to be welcomed as visitors to Cap'n's cabin. After about an hour's conference inside, I'd see Cap'n chasing chickens around his back yard until he caught three or four. Shortly after that, the visitors would depart from the streetcar stop and return to Paris laden with chickens, feet securely tied and squawking. My parents never commented about these events, and I took it that I shouldn't either.

During all those years, the most heart-rending tragedy had to do with Cap'n's little shepherd dog, Flu. She was without doubt the best trained cattle dog I ever saw, and to Cap'n she was like his right arm. Without her he would have a hard time rounding up cows and handling other livestock, which was a great part of his everyday work. As so often happens to dogs we love, Flu was running across the road in front of our house when she was struck by a car. The car never stopped, but it left the little dog lying in the road, her back apparently broken and her hind legs completely limp.

Cap'n saw the thing happen. He picked the dog up carefully in his arms and carried her to the cellar of our house, where he wrapped her in an old torn blanket. We all feared this was the end of Flu, meaning the loss of one of the most dedicated, hard-working members of the entire farm operation. Cap'n said nothing the rest of the day and very little for several days thereafter.

We fed Flu milk and bits from the table until it became clear that she had come to the end of her hard-working life. My father made the inescapable decision that she had to be destroyed. He asked Cap'n to carry out the fatal assignment. Flu disappeared from the cellar, and we thought that was it.

But several days later, I happened to be wandering, rifle in hand, across the pasture just south of our farmyard. I went to look at a sinkhole where we often threw junky things needing to be disposed of. When I got close, I saw Flu, still alive, her rear end beginning to decompose. Maggots were crawling out of her flanks. I didn't wait. I fired twice and turned my back not to look again. The deed was too much for a heart as warm and full of love as Cap'n's. We should have known that. It was our job to do.

As I grew older, I spent more of my time with the Redmons, the children of one of our tenant farmers. Though in a sense I grew away from the old black man, my respect and love for him didn't change. His honesty and devotion to the family were impossible to forget. Years later when I was away at law school in Cambridge, I got a letter from Mum. She told me that Cap'n had pneumonia and was in the hospital. Another letter came a few days later saying she had been at Cap'n's bedside when the old man died. He had always called Mum "Miss Julie." She said he had asked her, "Miss Julie, do you think God has forgive' me all my sins?" She said, "Yes, Cap'n, I know He has." She knew his sins were far smaller than those of the rest of us—mostly about young girls taking chickens back to Paris, or feeling rich on Saturdays at Bud Macon's pool hall.

Epilogue

Bourbon County has left its mark on me. The people of Bourbon County, some of whose lives were distant from mine and some who were closest to me—the Redmons, Cap'n, my brothers, and of course my mother and father—are a part of me now and will be forever. It has been said that if you want to live a long time, pick parents who lived a long time. By the same token, I suppose it could be said that if you want to be a good person, you should pick parents who are wonderful people. By that standard, I should be a better person than I am.

My early days seem far away now. I remember that our tobacco tenant's son, Willie Redmon, standing in the breeze rippling across the bluegrass pasture back of our main tobacco barn, would sometimes fall quiet. A cock would crow somewhere on the farm east of us, soon to be answered by one in Cap'n's chicken yard, then another behind us. A pause, and yet another could be heard far away in the distance. Willie always said if you'd be quiet for a moment anywhere on the farm, you could always hear a rooster crow.

Today we live in suburban Louisville where no roosters crow. If you pause a moment, you can usually hear a siren interrupting everything with its shout-down emergency message, or feel the deafening doppler noise of a helicopter spanking its way across the sky. There is sometimes the calm, summery hum of a power mower, but nothing so peaceful as one rooster calling to another from farm to farm.

Most of the old sounds are gone, and gone with them are the smells of the clover and honeysuckle of our front yard. Today's world is not like the world I remember, where in spring I could stand under blooming canopy of one of our apple trees and hear a hundred bees tending their business so that the tree itself was like a floral tuning fork sounding its A for the symphony of June.

That world is gone, locked up, sealed, like a box in the cornerstone of an old building about to be torn down to make a parking lot. No longer need I fear that, coming up the gravel driveway to Rocclicgan just before daybreak, I might wake up the mockingbird in the locust tree, whose burst of song would surely cause Mum to stir in her bed and begin worrying about me.

THE END